FREE TRIALS (AND TRIBULATIONS)

Kyle Racki
Free Trials and Tribulations

How to Build a Business While Getting Punched in the Mouth

Foreword by Dan Martell

COPYRIGHT © 2018 KYLE RACKI
All rights reserved.

FREE TRIALS (AND TRIBULATIONS)
How to Build a Business While Getting Punched in the Mouth

ISBN   978-1-5445-1358-4 *Paperback*
          978-1-5445-1357-7 *Ebook*

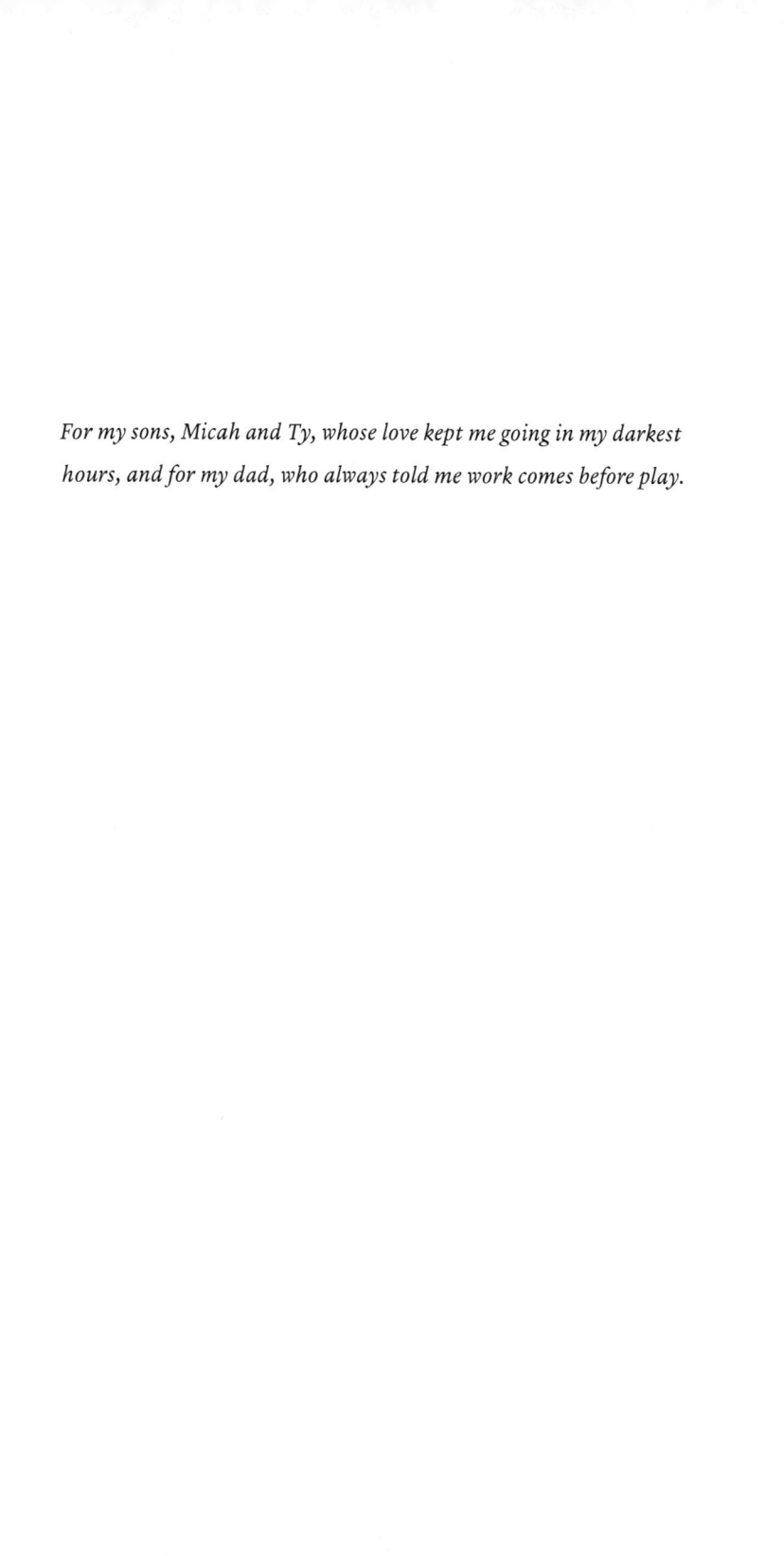

For my sons, Micah and Ty, whose love kept me going in my darkest hours, and for my dad, who always told me work comes before play.

CONTENTS

FOREWORD 11
PREFACE 17
INTRODUCTION 19

PART I: IN THE BEGINNING
1. FREELANCING IS A GATEWAY DRUG 33
2. LEAVING THE CABIN 59
3. THE AGENCY SHIT-SHOW 73

PART II: ARMAGEDDON
4. TINKERING WITH PRODUCTS 91
5. THE LORD TAKETH 109
6. KNOW WHEN TO FOLD 'EM 127

PART III: REBIRTH
7. THE TIDES CHANGE 143
8. BUILDING PRODUCT 151
9. FUELLING THE ROCKET SHIP 173
10. DEMAND 191
11. GROWTH 213
12. LEVELLING UP 233
13. FROM CHAOS TO CONQUEST 247

REFERENCES 257
ABOUT THE AUTHOR 259
ACKNOWLEDGMENTS 261

*Life is what happens to you while
you're busy making other plans.*

—JOHN LENNON, "BEAUTIFUL BOY"

FOREWORD

When I first met Kyle five years ago, I could tell he was different. The way he contributed to the startup community—by speaking at events, offering his advice to founders, and seeking mentorship of his own—signalled to me that he was going to stand out over the years as a pillar in his community.

Fast forward to today, and Kyle has created a multimillion-dollar software business that's being used by thousands of businesses around the world to help them close more business by empowering their sales force to communicate better with their customers.

When I met Kyle, I hadn't realized the incredible challenges he had to overcome to break free from his religion in order to live life on his own terms. Looking back now, it's probably the reason I connected with him and why his approach to life resonated with me.

When I was a teenager, I grew up in a crazy and intense environment as well. My mother was an alcoholic and my dad was always on the road travelling for work. I was diagnosed with ADHD at eleven years old and put on Ritalin. For many years I felt like I was broken. My self-esteem was nonexistent and I acted out at home. I was angry, and my parents couldn't handle me, so eventually they placed me in foster care.

Things spiralled out of control, and by the time I turned sixteen I had already been to jail twice. One day I was in a high-speed chase with the police and, after crashing the car, I tried to pull out a gun, thinking the police would take my life. As fate would have it, the police arrested me before I was able to get the gun.

Just like in Kyle's story, which you're about to read, I had hit rock bottom. It's incredible to me that Kyle decided to push forward and not let those situations give him reason to retreat and live a mediocre life. He may have hit a low point, but what I've learned over the years is that rock bottom can be a great foundation to rebuild your life.

It was in a remote rehab centre in the middle of the woods that I discovered a yellow book on Java programming and an old computer that literally saved my life. Learning how to code became my new addiction, and with the internet coming of age, it was the perfect canvas to build upon. The other gift I discovered as I started my first company was that entrepreneurship is the ultimate personal development program. It acts as a forcing function to become better in all other aspects of your life. If you're ever frustrated with your lack of business growth, the only place you need to look is in the mirror.

Since that time, I've been blessed to have started five companies (the first two were complete failures) but I grew the last three to multimillion-dollar companies and category leaders in their markets to eventual exits. I've also had the fortune of investing in forty-plus other software companies, like Intercom, Udemy, and Hootsuite, and speaking all over the world on entrepreneurship and growth.

Having gone through all of that, and now being on the other end, working with incredible founders like Kyle as a business coach, I've now come to learn that those who've gone through the most have the most to give.

I've discovered travelling the world, speaking with entrepreneurs, that many of them have gone through some kind of chaos or conflict in their childhood or early teen years. If I ask a room of a thousand entrepreneurs, 70 percent of the hands go up. I'm not saying that you need to have gone through hell in your childhood to build a big and meaningful company, but it definitely helps if you channel that energy appropriately.

For example, when Kyle was fourteen, his father, who struggled with alcoholism, had flown into a drunken rage and the entire neighbourhood heard it. He was so ashamed when he woke up that he took a bottle of sleeping pills to end his life, and ended up being taken to a mental health facility. When Kyle rode the school bus the next day, the neighbourhood bullies laughed at him and teased him about his drunken father. Kyle learned early on how to take a punch in the mouth, both literally and figuratively.

Learning to deal with chaos, knowing that you're the only person who's going to truly be responsible for your life, is a great gift to be given if you learn how to harness it. That's what Kyle shares in this book. How he's turned pain into progress, struggles into success, and failure into fortunes.

Being comfortable with chaos is what makes entrepreneurship the only option for many of us. In any other job, we fight with our coworkers, piss off our bosses, and get annoyed with how things are being done because we see a better way. When we get honest about our environment, our behaviour, and our beliefs, and start questioning how we've come to look at life, that's where the real opportunity lies to build something far greater than we ever thought possible. That misunderstood dichotomy is brought to life in the pages of this book.

Whether you're an entrepreneur deep in the trenches or still waiting on the sidelines, this book will bring you new insights, perspectives, and strategies that you'll be able to implement in your business today! Things like:

- How to get started as an entrepreneur and find your first customers without needing to raise money or take out a bank loan
- Why his agency business failed and how to create an agency you can sell
- How to launch your first SaaS product and build a product customers love
- How to create demand for your product and drive thousands of visitors to your website
- Why aiming high and hiring more employees is the key to major growth
- How to raise investment on your own terms and become wealthy before an exit
- How to level up and become a more effective leader for your staff

Kyle will teach you how to do all of this while dealing with the ups and downs life throws at you.

Over the years I've gotten to learn more about Kyle's background and how he's grown his business, shaped his life, and grown as an entrepreneur, father, and leader in his community. After reading the incredible stories he shares in this book, I know you'll draw inspiration you can use in your own life.

So as you devour this book and wear out your highlighter, be sure to remember that if you're going through hell, keep going.

You were destined for greatness, and hell on earth would be to meet the person you could have become.

It won't be easy, but take the punches and keep moving forward.

Never forget: no pressure, no diamonds.

Happy reading.

DAN MARTELL
Investor, Serial Entrepreneur, and Business Coach

PREFACE

As Forrest Gump, or rather, his momma, always said, "Life is like a box of chocolates: you never know what you're gonna get."

When I was a kid, I never thought I'd leave the Jehovah's Witnesses. On Tuesdays, Thursdays, and Sundays I would attend meetings at the Kingdom Hall. Every Saturday, I was knocking on strangers' doors, trying to place *Watchtower* and *Awake!* magazines. In fact, I was raised to believe that I would never reach adulthood in the world as we know it. Instead, God would intervene and bring about Armageddon by the time I graduated elementary school. From then on, I'd be living forever in a utopian earthly society made up of only Jehovah's Witnesses, where the so-called wicked (non-Witnesses) would be long dead and buried. It was a vaguely appealing, albeit morbid, future.

When I think about it now, I can't believe that was me. Fast-forward to the present: I'm thirty-five and the cofounder and CEO of a multimillion-dollar SaaS (software as a service) business. I get to wake up every morning and go to a job I love, doing work that's fun, challenging, and meaningful, with friends and colleagues whom I admire greatly. I often get to travel for work, attending conferences or meetings and seeing different parts of the world. On any given weekend, you'll find me at a boot camp class with my wife, Christina, or swimming in the ocean with my two sons. I may not be living that immortal life, but it's a hell of a lot happier and more fulfilling than where my life was heading just a few short years ago.

So, what happened? Somewhere in my mid-twenties, I underwent a metamorphosis—profound, painful, and unexpected—sparked by tragedy and failure. I wrote this book as a way to document what happened and to provide some lessons and hope to entrepreneurs in the midst of their own despair, so, like me, they can rise like a phoenix from the ashes of their mistakes and build the life and business they want for themselves.

INTRODUCTION

Entrepreneurship is hot right now.

We're living in a unique time, when entrepreneurs are viewed in the same vein as rappers, actors, and athletes. Jeff Bezos is called a "style icon" by the *New York Times*. Paparazzi snap pics of Elon Musk arm-in-arm with his indie pop-musician girlfriend, Grimes. Fans stop Gary Vaynerchuk on the streets of New York to get a selfie. Entrepreneurs are more rock stars than *actual rock stars*.

This is a very recent thing. We're living in an era unlike any generation before us, because the internet makes it relatively easy to become an entrepreneur. Within minutes you can have an e-commerce store up and running on Shopify. Learning a programming framework, such as node.js or Ruby on Rails, makes coding and deploying your own software somewhat approachable, and Amazon provides a cheap and powerful cloud hosting infrastructure. Meanwhile, Facebook allows you to cost-effectively market your business to billions of potential customers. It doesn't matter where you live; you can build a remote team from anywhere and collaborate via Slack.

ENTREPRENEURSHIP ISN'T SEXY

Due to this ease of entry, the internet has also created a legion of fake entrepreneurs. They pose next to Beamers they don't own and post the picture to Instagram. They have hundreds of thousands of "followers," mostly made up of purchased bots. They focus more on *looking* the part, rather than putting their heads down and building sustainable businesses that can withstand an economic downturn. Some even raise millions of dollars in venture capital and subsequently set it on fire because they don't understand the fundamentals of business: supply and demand, unit economics, and how to extract revenue from customers.

The truth is, real entrepreneurship isn't sexy. Behind the curtain, it doesn't show well on Instagram: the wins and losses, the emotional roller coaster, the ecstasy followed by depression, the pissed off customers and employees, the troubled relationships and the crushing debt, and the late-night grind sessions while everyone else around you watches Netflix and chills. Here's the worst part: *nobody cares*. Nobody feels bad for you. In fact, because you're "self-employed," they all think you're rich and have it made. "Wow, I wish I was my own boss and could give myself a raise and do whatever I wanted all the time!" Insert sad trombone sound.

It takes a tremendous amount of focus, dedication, and endurance to be a successful entrepreneur, and even then it's not guaranteed. When bad shit happens, inside or outside the business, it can take away the focus you need. If you dig deeply into any entrepreneur's story, you'll almost always find that they succeeded by hunkering down to keep going, even when all the signs pointed to giving up.

There's really no way around it: to be successful, you have to learn how to take a punch in the mouth, or several at once, and carry on. Life knocked me around quite a bit on the way to successful entrepreneurship, so let my story serve as proof that you can take the punches and still come out on top, no matter where you start.

MY LEAP INTO FREELANCING

I never intended to build a big business. My goals and aspirations were pretty modest. I started my career working in an advertising agency as a graphic designer when I was nineteen years old. After a few years, I noticed that some of my older colleagues were quitting the agency life and going out on their own as freelancers. I was intrigued, thinking you had to be some sort of genius to pull this off, but as I talked to them, I discovered it wasn't that big a leap. The agency charged a certain amount for our work, so all it took to go freelance was to cut out the middleman and charge a little bit less. That meant managing clients directly, but I had a pretty good head for relationships. Besides, I had seen how my bosses operated, and I was often amazed at how little business leadership skill seemed necessary to own and run an agency. I was young and cocky and thought I could do better.

The more I thought about it, the better freelancing sounded. It actually seemed to fit perfectly into my life at the time. I was a rising member of the Jehovah's Witnesses, the church (or cult, as I would ultimately come to see it) that I grew up in. I had taken on the role of *ministerial servant* in the church—kind of like a deacon or elder-in-training—and gave talks at the Kingdom Hall, organized the preaching territory, and was generally seen as an upstanding, spiritual young man. At twenty years old, I already had a wife and six-year-old stepdaughter.[1] If I were self-employed, I could entertain the idea of being a *pioneer*—someone who dedicates fifty to sixty hours a

---

1   It's common among Jehovah's Witnesses and other fundamentalist groups for members to get married at very young ages because fornication—sex outside of marriage—is forbidden. And, well, nineteen-year-olds really want to have sex.

month to preaching work. Most pioneers earn their living in part-time or contract work, usually as office cleaners, so they can devote more time to preaching. As a freelancer, I would be able to make my own hours and have more time in my schedule for my work as a pioneer.

That's not what happened. As soon as I went out on my own and started freelancing, I found a lot of excuses to not go out on field service: I needed to be with my first son, Micah, who was less than a year old. I was too busy with client work. These demands on my time were real, but mostly I hated knocking on doors and pushing religion on people. It quickly became clear to me that the real reason I'd left the agency wasn't to have more time for field service. Although I didn't know it yet, I was taking my first steps toward waking up from my cult indoctrination and finding my true calling. My actual escape from the Witnesses wouldn't happen for a few years to come.

THE HELL STORM COMETH

I loved being a freelance web designer and developer. I quickly brought in an abundance of client work, and more than doubled my salary that year. At the last agency I had worked at, I made $38,000 a year. Once I quit and went out on my own in March 2008, I grossed around $80,000. Not bad for a twenty-four-year-old. Things went so well that I started my own agency and began hiring people. But life began to unravel pretty quickly soon afterward.

In 2009, my relationship with my first wife, Paula, fell apart in a big way. She became addicted to sleeping pills, and attempted suicide twice. She physically attacked me, and police were called on multiple occasions.[2] Things were so chaotic that we separated that year for the first, but not final, time. I moved out of the family home and was living in a small run-down apartment. Paula once showed up at the office and, in front of all my staff, demanded to be paid for her 1 percent share in the business, and left only after my business partner threatened to call the police. A year later, my agency business was in a bad place. We barely had enough money to make ends meet, and were in debt to the bank for $150,000. The CRA[3] froze my personal bank account as I struggled to pay back taxes I'd racked up as a freelancer. Then came 2012, the beginning of two years of hell that upturned my life. The punches just kept coming.

The year prior, my father was diagnosed with hepatitis C, a disease he had been carrying, unrecognized, for thirty years, which gradually destroyed his liver. A year later, I

---

[2] I personally believe Paula has undiagnosed borderline personality disorder, which makes normal, peaceful relationships almost impossible. Even though we're now divorced, she is still in an almost constant state of chaos, and co-parenting with her is extremely difficult.

[3] Canada Revenue Agency, like the Canadian version of the Internal Revenue Service in the United States.

sat by his bed at home as he drew his final breath. I was already having religious doubts, but only then did I realize how hollow were the attempts by well-meaning church members to comfort me. I began waking up from years of indoctrination and stopped suppressing my doubts.

My father's death was a catalyst. It triggered an avalanche of rebellious feelings that had been building for years. As a teenager, I was already breaking the rules. I was looked upon as a rebel by other members of the religion, someone to be avoided by the good kids who followed the rules. I was Bart Simpson to their Rodd and Todd, so to speak. I didn't go to many church meetings. I played in a rock band with worldly schoolmates.[4] I drank alcohol and smoked marijuana.

I had always felt like an outsider, yet I still believed in the religion. The Watchtower (the governing body) tells you that God's going to kill you in Armageddon if you don't fall in line. So I changed my ways. I doubled down and applied myself to the faith.

It wasn't until years later, when I was in the midst of running my agency business, that I once again stopped performing my church duties. I was no longer a regular

---

4 "Wordly," as used in the Jehovah's Witnesses, is a negative term that refers to any non-Witness. Witnesses are urged not to spend any unnecessary time socializing with worldly people. It's common among cults to employ loaded language and have their own definitions for common words, such as Scientology's use of the term "suppressive person."

at meetings and field service, and I didn't study the Bible and Watchtower materials as I was expected to. Because of my marital difficulties, I was labelled "spiritually weak" and I was publicly removed as a ministerial servant.

The hell storm in my personal and professional life was changing me in ways I'd never imagined. Shortly after my father's death, I gave myself permission to read the writings of former Jehovah's Witnesses, also known as *apostates*. I'd had doubts for a long time, but now the cracks were getting wider, and I began to look at the religion more objectively.

LIFTING THE VEIL

Leaving the Witnesses is a story in itself, and one I'll tell in chapter 5. It was extremely painful to leave, but it was also immensely freeing. It was like breaking out of a mental prison I had been captive in since birth. Once you escape, everything becomes clearer; it's like a veil has been lifted from your eyes. Leaving the church was traumatic, but it set me free to rebuild my life the way I wanted. I learned how the world really worked and how to choose who I wanted as friends and family.

I may not have had the easiest road, but I know others who've had it far worse. I'm extremely grateful for my struggles, as they shaped who I am. One of the many things I learned through my experience as a Jehovah's Witness is resilience—there's nothing like going door-to-door, getting yelled at, and having doors slammed in your face to teach you how to eat shit and deal with it. Vital lessons for anyone who goes into business.

BECOMING AN ENTREPRENEUR

Leaving the religion didn't magically make my life better, at least not right away. I still had a failing business and a tumultuous marriage. Yet it was the beginning of my path to self-reliance and entrepreneurship.

In a few years I managed to go from near-bankruptcy to a multimillion-dollar business. I've now got the financial security and freedom I've always wanted. As much as possible, I've removed from my life the people who caused me misery. I found true love in my best friend, Christina, whom I married in 2018, and I'm the proud dad of my sons, Micah and Ty. I'm respected in the local startup community; entrepreneurs want to take me out for coffee and find out how I did it.

I did it by starting a company called Proposify. It's a SaaS (software as a service) product that streamlines the process of creating business proposals to win work. The idea grew out of my own frustrations. Back in the mid-2000s, we were still burning files to CDs and emailing Word docs around. There was no Dropbox at that time. I envisioned a solution to that logistical nightmare, something like Basecamp for proposals. I sketched it out, but sat on it for years.

If I'd had a crystal ball and could have seen where things would end up—VCs contacting me every day to invest or to try to acquire the business—I never would have believed it. We're now approaching $10 million annual recurring revenue, with over fifty employees and many thousands of customers around the world.

CORE LESSONS AND STRATEGIES

I wrote this book because I know that running a business can be a lonely experience. Being an entrepreneur may look glamorous, but it's not. I want other entrepreneurs to know they're not alone in their struggles. Everyone's personal experience is different. We all endure our own trials in life, but we also have much in common in our striving for economic independence.

I mentor entrepreneurs, talking them through the anxiety, stress, and hard choices they face. My goal with this book is to expand that conversation to a broader audience. By documenting all the crazy things that happened to me over the years, I hope to distill the core lessons I learned and offer them to other businesspeople. If you're going through a personal crisis while running your business, I hope my experiences will help you see that there's always a light at the end of the tunnel. If you're just starting a business, or wondering how to grow one, chances are I've been in your shoes, too.

In addition to sharing my story, I'll share key tactical lessons and strategies I've learned creating products, selling to customers, and scaling a company. Endurance alone doesn't guarantee a win. At the end of the day, you have to do the right things to build a business that generates the wealth you need to live the life you want. I'll be sharing every major business mistake I made and giving you a sneak peek behind the curtain at how I started and grew Proposify.

We'll start at the beginning of my journey to entrepreneurship—my first steps at becoming a freelancer. I invite you to come with me, compare notes, and build your own business along the way.

PART I

IN THE BEGINNING

CHAPTER ONE

FREELANCING IS A GATEWAY DRUG

When I was fourteen, a family friend invested $10,000 of his own money to open a used clothing store called Wear-It-Again. Lloyd was proud of his venture, but my dad, who loved teasing his friends, openly referred to the business as The Skid Mark.

My friend Darryl helped his father out at the store, and I'd visit him there. I was fascinated by the idea of opening a business and what goes into it. Yet it was no surprise to me that my father belittled the store; my family had always expressed the opinion that starting a business was too risky. Eventually, when the store did close down, they dogmatically shrugged their shoulders, with an "I told you so" demeanour.

BUSINESS IS RISKY

My parents were the opposite of risk-takers. Their attitude was that building a successful business wasn't within reach of mere mortals like us. People like us take the safe route, working for somebody else and earning a steady paycheque. Like my parents, most people seek a regular full-time job because they want a feeling of security. Unfortunately, the reality is that it's just a feeling. Your boss can fire you or lay you off at any moment. The days of working twenty-five years at a company and retiring with a gold watch are long behind us.

The unavoidable truth is that new businesses *are* risky. They often require upfront capital and years of toiling before they begin to show a profit. But what if there were an easier way to dip your toes into the waters of entrepreneurship without taking on so much risk? It turns out there is, and it's well within reach of almost anyone.

CHANGING TIMES, NEW OPPORTUNITIES

During the past ten years, there has been a measurable shift to a freelancing mindset. The number of freelancers, independent consultants, and contractors working from home and remotely has risen dramatically.

Since 2014, the US freelance workforce has grown three times faster than the overall US workforce, from 53 million in 2014 to 57.3 million this year. That's 8.1 percent growth compared to 2.6 percent for the overall workforce. By 2027, freelancers are expected to make up the majority of the US workforce, based on growth rates witnessed over the past year.

Risk doesn't seem to worry these people, and that makes sense to me. Going freelance doesn't really entail any more risk than working at a job where you might get fired or laid off during a recession or if the company fails. As the numbers demonstrate, so-called job security is becoming a bit of an old-fashioned concept.

In fact, we all take risks every day. It's part of life. You take some level of risk just walking out your door—a meteor could land on your head—but you can't live your life worrying about everything that could possibly go wrong.

For many people, freelancing is the first step on the path to entrepreneurship. It brings more benefits than risk. As a freelancer, it's relatively easy to get clients in the door. You have very low overhead and you don't need to bring in huge amounts of work to live a good lifestyle, pay your bills, and make some profit.

All you need to get started is a skill that people need and are willing to pay for and, of course, your first client. As long as you do a good job with that client, it's relatively easy to get the second one and to jump out on your own.

Is entrepreneurship really much different than freelancing? Is it riskier? Many people see it that way. An employee once told me that she admired entrepreneurs for being risk-takers; she confided that she didn't think she could ever run her own business. She knew she was a great manager who could lead and scale teams, but entrepreneurship seemed too big a leap.

Maybe that was once true, but it's much less so now. Being an entrepreneur used to mean opening a retail shop with a lease, buying equipment, hiring an agency to design a logo, and paying out thousands of dollars in advertising. It involved taking out bank loans and maybe putting your house up as collateral. That *was* risky. However, times have changed. The internet lets you tinker, experiment, and test the market easily and cheaply without putting yourself in danger. For example, the crafty among us can sell their wares on a website like Etsy while working on their nine-to-five. If their products take off, they can quit and go full time into their business. A friend of mine named Sarah Hart started a business selling webinars and very quickly grew a six-figure income from a one-woman business she operates at home. There's much less peril in going out on your own now than ever before.

THE OLD HUSTLE AND GRIND

I started out working a "safe" job as a designer in an agency, but I quickly discovered that I couldn't thrive there. I had a youthful passion and confidence the bosses wouldn't tolerate; they certainly didn't allow a twenty-three-year-old to tell them what was and wasn't a good idea for a client strategy. I didn't just want to earn a steady paycheque, I wanted to be the best at what I did and earn an income that reflected it. I knew I needed to spread my wings, and working for someone else just wasn't cutting it.

I worked full time at the agency when my son, Micah, was still just a newborn. To prepare for my exit from the agency, I fit in freelance work after my son was in bed and on the weekends. I had a couple of small clients who'd given me design work or websites to build. I wasn't paid much at the agency, so these projects brought some money in the door and started to build my clientele. I worked that way for a year, at close to fourteen hours a day.

I was overwhelmed, and so was my family. To her credit, Paula supported me going out on my own and offered to take a waitressing job to bring in some extra money so I could quit my nine-to-five. She was getting sick of me working so much, but I wasn't quite ready to take the leap into freelancing exclusively. Luckily, one of my coworkers, Kevin, provided an excellent sounding board while I tried to make a decision. We used to frequent the gelato shop downstairs from the office to get coffee. Kevin was in business development, about twenty years older than me, and I'd bounce ideas off him (like my crazy idea for proposal software, which he thought was brilliant).

I was contemplating quitting the nine-to-five, but wasn't sure I'd have enough freelance work to provide for my young family. Kevin had been an entrepreneur most of his life, and had only recently begun working full time for someone else, as he was in the process of immigrating to Canada. One of the things he always told me is "There's no reward without risk and sacrifice." That advice helped motivate me. Everyone wants the reward, but few are willing to sacrifice and take risks. Understanding that concept is what made me quit my full-time job and go freelance. Later, he joined me, and he's been my partner for over a decade, across two businesses.

TAKING THE LEAP

I was ready—but that didn't mean it would be easy. I had envisioned building up so much freelance work that I could easily quit my job and double my salary. I was looking for a nice, easy, smooth transition, but it never materialized. Until you focus on something full time, it's hard to succeed. So, with Paula's support, I just did it—I quit my nine-to-five. I had one freelance job contracted at that time. It paid $3,500, which was about how much I cleared every month at the agency. That meant I had one month to complete the work while hustling to get more clients. It worked. With complete focus on freelancing, I quickly had more clients coming in the door and was able to make enough money to pay rent and keep my family fed.

Not only did I enjoy success as a freelancer, I learned about the value of being willing to take a risk. To this day, I keep that lesson in mind when my company is testing or experimenting with a new marketing channel or tweaking our pricing. Most people would rather stick with the status quo than risk failure by changing something, and it's something I often have to push members of my team on. However, you don't get any reward in life without taking some risk.

Gary Vaynerchuk has said that he knew he was wired for business by the age of six, when he was not only selling lemonade on the sidewalk every summer day, but convincing his friends to sell lemonade *for him* while he collected his percentage of the profits. He was a born hustler.

I wasn't quite like that. I was the kid sitting inside, drawing superheroes, getting in trouble for drawing caricatures of my teachers during class. As I mentioned, I also grew up in an environment that heavily discouraged entrepreneurship. However, some salesmanship seeds were planted early on by the Jehovah's Witnesses.

MY FIRST PROVING GROUND

I spent many a Saturday going door-to-door, preaching to strangers. I learned how to handle rejection, because I was selling a product that most people didn't want. I couldn't get out of it; I had to knock on every door and try. So I got a lot of practice. If there's a silver lining in being raised a Jehovah's Witness, it was the weekly sales and public speaking training.[5] Even the tactics for trying to sell the church's literature were similar to sales. At our meetings on Tuesday nights, we learned to sell effectively through role-play. We learned how to find common ground with the "householder" who opened the door, not by being argumentative, but rather by identifying their pain points, and by using teaching techniques, such as metaphors to illustrate key messages or contrast to compare positives and negatives.

As a result of this training, I was the only kid in my class who could give a presentation or stand up and speak comfortably about how my summer went. I was the only one

---

5   I've learned that in recent years Jehovah's Witnesses have discontinued the "Theocratic Ministry School" where they teach public speaking. This saddens me, because the speaking and teaching training is one of the few practical benefits children receive by being in the religion.

who wouldn't shake or sway while I spoke. I was used to it because I had to stand in front of one hundred grown-ups every month and deliver a five- or ten-minute Bible talk. I'd be graded on stage in front of the audience by an adult who'd offer feedback and suggestions, like working on my sense stress and modulation. Try asking any other eight-year-old what sense stress and modulation is.

Other early training came from taking over a friend's paper route. My friend and Skid Mark employee, Darryl, was a few years older than me and was so nerdy he made Steve Urkel look like his cool alter-ego, Stefan Urquelle. Darryl owned every console ever made, from the Commodore 64 to the Sega Dreamcast. He had literally covered an entire room in his parents' basement with Transformers and anime figures, from ceiling to floor, a room I called his shrine. How could he afford all this? It turned out his newspaper route made him around $500 a month, which was a lot of money to me at the time.

It became my mission to inherit Darryl's paper route when he outgrew it. When he turned eighteen, I told him I wanted to take it on, and I did, for three years. Before then, I'd had to play Super Mario 64 on the displays at Blockbuster until they told me to leave. With the money I earned delivering papers, I could finally afford my own Nintendo 64. It was life-changing.

A newspaper route is the perfect training ground for a young entrepreneur. It's very different than cashiering at McDonald's or working retail, where you're told what to do by a supervisor. A paper route is a model for running a business. I had my own customers, and every month I collected payment from them in person. I entered the amounts in a ledger where I had to account for every penny and make sure all the numbers added up. Instead of issuing a paycheque, the paper company withdrew money from my account. It was pretty close to running a business.

If I wanted more customers, it was up to me to knock on doors and ask people if they wanted a paper subscription. I could fill the funnel and deliver as much as I was able to sell. If I wanted to stay behind after school and jam with my band, I would have to find someone to cover for me and pay them for it. I learned something about hiring and managing people, plus shouldering the responsibility for making sure the work got done every day, no matter what. In a way, taking on that paper route was a gutsy move, given how much my family discouraged business ventures.

LEANING INTO MY STRENGTHS

It still seemed a bit of a stretch to think of myself as a businessperson. I was always the artsy kid who loved to draw, not the hustler. I started drawing early. My mother proudly told other people that when I was three years old I brought her a drawing of Ernie and Bert that looked exactly like the characters on *Sesame Street*. In fact, at first she thought my older sister, Erica, had drawn it, given her being three and a half years older than me, but a quick test proved that Erica's attempt at recreating the artwork made her an unlikely source.

I was always drawing. I didn't create much fine art, mind you, but I had scribblers full of superheroes, some pre-existing and others of my own creation. I also made caricatures of my teachers to entertain my classmates. None of them were very flattering, but they got a lot of giggles from the other sixth graders. Several earned me trips to the principal's office, (particularly the one I drew of our music teacher's fart blowing all the kids away).

When I got into high school, I took art more seriously. I took a 3-D digital art class and aced it. It was one of the only classes in which I earned a 95 percent grade. (My math grade was closer to 60 percent, English was 72 percent, and I flunked out of auto mechanics with a 22 percent. Don't ever let me try to change your oil.)

My art teacher, Mr. Simoni, nurtured my talent and helped me look at different college programs. I had my eye on a private school, but my parents weren't well-off, so that seemed unlikely. To my surprise, Mr. Simoni recommended the community college. He said I would get better training there, and I'd learn core design skills the expensive school wouldn't cover.

Mr. Simoni was a smart man. I went to Nova Scotia Community College and thrived, even as a seventeen-year-old kid taking classes with thirty- or forty-year-olds. I had been pretty sheltered all my life; this was the first time I was exposed to people from different backgrounds and perspectives. The classes—semiotics, media studies, art history—gave me my first real taste of critical thinking. I also discovered graphic design. I was beginning to realize how interesting the world was, compared to the limited life I'd led in the Jehovah's Witnesses.

GETTING HIRED

As graduation day neared, I was in a panic. All of my classmates, who had come back to college to learn skills that would land them in new careers, would be in the job market, too. With all these new grads out there in the workforce, would there be enough work in the city for me to get a job? Why would anyone hire a nineteen-year-old?

Imposter syndrome struck hard; I was young and didn't feel I was good enough. I hustled and contacted dozens of agencies, to no avail. I also looked for any freelance work

I could get, including restaurant menus and charity newsletters. It was still a few months before graduation, but I was getting desperate when Rick Smith, the art director at Impact, emailed me with the subject line "Come on down."

I wasn't expecting to meet with a long-haired, thirty-something hipster in a Hawaiian shirt, but there he was, looking at my portfolio and loving it. I was offered a one-month internship at the ad agency as part of my school curriculum. It was a huge step up for me. I was in the door. Instead of selling Shania Twain CDs all day at Music World, I got to work on a Mac, creating billboards and logos with other designers. It was my "pinch me, I must be dreaming" moment.

My goal was to get hired on after the month, so I made myself indispensable. I pitched in on all the crap none of the other designers wanted to do, like editing a menu for a restaurant client using Quark Express on the boss's PC and creating PowerPoint presentations for the salespeople. At the end of the month, they offered me a part-time position at an hourly rate. I may have been making only ten dollars an hour, but I was no longer an imposter. I was a professional designer now.

MOVING UP

I worked at Impact all summer and loved it. It led to my first full-time, salaried position at a publishing company called Holiday Media. I had high hopes and expectations.

Impact was closer to the ad agency stereotype: all styled with hardwood flooring and brick walls, people zipping around on scooters and playing Ping-Pong, calling themselves "creatives." Holiday Media looked more like the American version of *The Office*. It was depressing, with employees sitting in grey cubicles, and fluorescent lights shining down on bottomless stacks of paper. The boss made inappropriate jokes that no one laughed at. My first enemy was a designer who looked and acted just like the Dwight character on the television show. I really hated that guy.

It was enough of a shock to make me beg and plead my way back to Impact. After a year at *The Office*, I reentered the fold at Impact and worked there happily for two years, meeting many of the people I work with today. Two years later, I moved to another small agency, called Modern Media, where I met Kevin and began working on my exit plan to go freelance.

FREELANCE FREEDOM

My first freelance days put me in a new panic. I was terrified that I wouldn't get enough design work, so I tried to make myself as versatile as possible. I could see that the demand for web developers was growing faster than the demand for designers, so I decided to do both. Clients were paying huge money for animated Flash sites. That meant a whole lot of learning—I studied all the time, and even took a book on ActionScript on vacation to Florida with me—and it opened up my options. If I couldn't get design work, I could code, and vice versa.

I didn't realize I was making my way toward entrepreneurship by freelancing, but it was the first step. I took on some bad clients and projects, like designing lightning bolt decals for a guy's pickup truck and getting ripped off. I had a lot to learn about doing business. In addition to developing my designing and programming skills, I had to learn how to invoice clients, how to write proposals, and how to close sales. That's when the idea for Proposify started to form.

Freelancing was the gateway drug to entrepreneurship. Each successful project left me eager to climb higher and work at the next level. Freelancing is not for everyone—it can get lonely—but it excited me because I love learning, and as a freelancer, I was always learning.

I rarely had trouble bringing in clients; it's amazing how quickly you can find freelance work if you have any sort of network. Most people don't realize it and opt for uninteresting part-time jobs instead. One of my past employees—a developer—actually took a weekend job at the mall to help pay for his wedding. He didn't realize he could make much more money using his development skills to freelance after work and on weekends than by manning a kiosk at the mall.

My advice? Go out and convince businesses that you can take some work off their overloaded plates. Small coding, design, or writing projects won't provide long-term stability, but they can bring in some money when you need it. I say take all the freelance work you can get, and do it well. The experience will give you a step up into entrepreneurship.

HOW TO GET STARTED

One reality check for the new freelancer: if you've just gotten out of school, you don't know anything yet. You lack the experience to deliver the quality of work that clients expect from a professional. You need to grow your skills until you're not only competent but significantly better than your competition. To do that, you need to work in a staff position where you can learn the job under a mentor.

FIND A MENTOR

I once saw Gordon Ramsay on TV talking about how much he learned working under master chefs in Paris. They made clear the consequences for getting it wrong: if he screwed up, the chefs threw frying pans in his direction. Next time, he didn't screw up. The experience probably wasn't easy but it gave him the chops he needed to become Chef Ramsay.

As a designer, I got my experience working at two agencies and a publishing company for four and a half years in total. In both jobs, I was guided by experienced designers who had much better skills than I had. There's nothing like working under a highly skilled art director to give a designer the experience he or she needs. I remember Rick getting angry with me when I retouched an ad campaign on the smallest version of the Photoshop file, instead of on the largest version. My approach, a rookie mistake, meant I'd need to redo the work when it came time to turn the ad into a billboard. Rick was right for calling me out on it, and I had to redo it all. He probably would have thrown a pan at me if one was within reach. I never forgot that lesson.

On another occasion, I had to design an invitation for a Christmas-themed event. I felt guilty doing the work because, as a Jehovah's Witness, I didn't celebrate Christmas (as a child I had to opt out of all holiday-related activities and concerts). After Rick reviewed my design, he offered some harsh criticism. I responded, "Well, I don't even celebrate Christmas." He fired back, "Do you celebrate good design?"

SET UP SHOP

When you're ready, it's time to launch your freelancing business. It's much easier to get started as a freelancer than as an entrepreneur. Entrepreneurs have to make significant upfront investments and often raise large sums of money before they can even begin to build a product.

The freelancer, on the other hand, can start making money on day one. You don't have to rent office space and hire employees. These days, you don't even need a permanent location. It doesn't matter if you work from home or a café, as long as you can be productive. All you need to do is get one client to PayPal you some money.

If you do high-quality work for that client, they will refer other people to you, so you don't need to do much marketing or sales work. When I started out, I found that focusing on choosing the right clients and delivering on the work meant I had a steady stream of clients. In fact, I often had too many clients asking to work with me; instead of worrying about having enough work, I ended up wondering how I would fit it all in.

To find clients, you simply have to pinpoint a problem people have that you can solve. Whatever you do, someone needs you to do it for them. What can you do for people that will make it worthwhile for them to pay you? If you're experienced in accounting, legal services, writing, designing, marketing, coding, or any number of professions, people will pay for your help. You just have to find those people.

> **WHAT ABOUT FREELANCE JOB SITES?**
>
> If sales is not your strong suit, you can use services like Upwork or 99designs to find clients but be aware that quality varies. Many sites are nothing but a race to the bottom, where you compete with other people willing to work for cheap. If you live in a developed country, you can't begin to compete with people in less developed countries who charge a low hourly rate. You might even be asked to do speculative work without upfront pay. I don't recommend it.
>
> I don't think any of these big services are doing it for the workers; they're not trying to create a great lifestyle for their contractors. They're building a big engine, and as soon as they can automate it with robots, they will.
>
> So, while you can get some work this way, your best bet is to train yourself in sales. If you're bad at sales, it's time to learn it, get good at it, and build those relationships.

SET YOUR FEES

Once you find your clients and meet with them, you'll need to figure out what to charge. New freelancers tend to charge too little because they calculate an hourly wage based on their previous salary, without realizing they were giving their old boss a volume discount on their time. That doesn't work when you're selling your time in small chunks. As a freelancer, you have to put a premium on those hours. It's often appropriate to double or triple your previous hourly rate.

Often, a per-project fee can be more appropriate than an hourly rate. Project fees often serve both parties best, allowing you to work efficiently and giving the client the peace of mind that comes with knowing how much the project will cost. When you charge by the project, everyone knows what the bottom line is. I remember that for a simple website design, I could charge $2,000; little did the client know that I could slam out the work in only two or three hours, and the clients loved the designs. I could literally make $1,000 an hour on certain jobs!

Many people feel uncomfortable talking about their fees and prices. Money is an off-limits topic in our personal lives, but in business, money is anything but taboo. It's the official language of every business transaction. As you mature as a freelancer, you'll likely get more comfortable talking about money; you have to, because it's the engine that keeps your whole world running.

GET PAID

Once you've asked for a fair fee and the client has accepted, it's time to dive in and do the work, right? Yes, but don't take a deep dive just yet. If you work first, then deliver the work, then ask to get paid, you're asking for trouble. Too many freelancers get burned by clients who quibble about details to avoid paying, or don't pay at all.

The transaction should work in reverse: get paid, do the work, then deliver it. Think about what you expect as a customer. When you go to McDonald's and order a McGriddle (you probably should eat fewer McGriddles), you place the order, pay, then get your food. That's the way it should work for the person hiring you to do freelance work. Don't do all the work first and hope to get a cheque in thirty days—get paid first. You don't have to insist on full payment up front; you can ask for a partial payment to begin, another payment midway through, and one upon delivery. You can also offer monthly payments to regulate cash flow for the client and add stability for yourself. Just make sure you get paid.

DELIVER THE GOODS

Finally, the moment of truth—delivering the carefully crafted product to the client. My motto for handing over the goods: under-promise and over-deliver. Doing the opposite is a huge mistake.

You've probably been on the client end of a business relationship that over-promises and under-delivers, so you know how frustrating it can be. I've had a similar experience building a house with a contractor. When we began the process, the designer told us she was going to send us the first round of designs on a Monday. When Monday rolled around with no sign of the designs, we sent an email asking when they were coming. She didn't respond by sending them; she suggested we plan to meet the following week instead. That one change threw off our whole timeline and didn't make us likely to refer people to this designer in the future.

With your clients, tell them what they *don't* want to hear first—that the project will take longer than they thought, or it will cost more, or that you can't deliver everything they want, whatever it is. If you manage to finish before the deadline or come in under budget, you look like a hero. But if you tell them what they want to hear and fail to fulfill it, or fail to communicate the problem, that client is not coming back. If you have customer service staff, under-promise and over-deliver is a good philosophy to impart to them.

FIND THE TIME

Taking the steps necessary to launch a successful freelance business can be time-consuming, and most freelancers face the challenge of finding enough time to do it all. If you think about how you actually spend your time, though, you might find it relatively easy to free up a few hours every day. Instead of sitting on the couch every evening catching up on the latest television shows, you could be slamming through work or returning a client's email. Most people have time available to work on their business—they just need to dedicate the time. If you want to succeed as a freelancer or an entrepreneur, get comfortable sacrificing most of the hours you used to spend on relaxation; instead, put it into improving your craft, learning the business, getting clients, and doing the work.

That's what I did while I worked at Modern Media. I worked into the evenings and on weekends, read programming books on vacation, and immersed myself in the field. I thought that would change when I went full time into freelancing. It didn't. I was still working 24/7, but not because I had to. I did it because I liked it.

NURTURE YOUR NETWORK

Even working all the time, I didn't just hole up in my office. I also took time to meet people and expand my network. I didn't make a conscious decision to benefit from the relationships I was developing, but in time, I did. Relationships tend to pay dividends in the future, so whether you're talking with people you meet at conferences, colleagues you work with, or potential clients, you have to get out there and make those connections. They're the ones who will refer new business your way.

Maintaining your network can be a little harder as a freelancer, because you don't see your colleagues every day as you might in a full-time position. When I left the agency to go freelance, I would stay in touch by asking my former coworkers out for coffee or lunch every now and then. I'm glad I kept those connections; as it turns out I'm still working with people I met at Impact back in 2003.

BRAINSTORM AND TINKER

Just as you never know whom you'll be working with down the line, you can't predict what concepts you'll come across in your work that might spark a new idea. In my very first jobs, I realized how important proposals were to a business. I went in thinking that meeting a client about a project was the big win; I soon understood it was only the first step. The next step, the proposal, is what ultimately sells them on your company.

One client we had at Impact stands out in particular—Stright-MacKay, a marine parts distributor. I was a junior designer at the time, so I wasn't working on the content, but I was working with the account managers who were writing the proposal. As we worked late every night to get the proposal out by the deadline, I saw how chaotic and stressful this process was. I felt there had to be a better way, and it led me to brainstorming a solution.

By 2006, I realized business development representatives were in dire need of a streamlined way to handle proposals. When Basecamp's project management software became popular, I was inspired to tinker away at some software ideas specifically for projects that required proposals. It's what eventually propelled me into founding Proposify.

TAKE THE LEAP

Everyone should give freelancing or consulting a try; most people find it life-changing. The freedom and flexibility can be incredibly satisfying. True, there's an element of risk. Getting started as a freelancer is unlikely to be the seamless transition you hope for. Everyone hopes they'll quickly build up a client base and make so much money moonlighting that it'll be easy to quit their full-time job. That rarely happens. You're more likely to face a gap—a point where you have less money coming in than you need—but if you take that leap, you can make it to the other side.

If you wait for circumstances to be perfect, you may be waiting forever.

CHAPTER TWO

—

LEAVING THE CABIN

Here's what the leap can look like.

On my last day at the agency and my first morning as a freelancer, I woke up with a thrill—part exuberance, part terror. I was free to do my own thing! However, I also had a family and a rented house and a seven-month-old baby and personal debt, and I didn't have a job. I hadn't saved any money before going out on my own, so I had to get clients in the door—right away.

My first client was a property management firm called Rentals Your Way, an Airbnb precursor. The job was a web build, nothing special, but it paid $3,500—exactly what I needed to make in my first month.

With that, I was off. That month, I attended a local marketing conference. A few days later, agencies and individuals started sending me work, and I said yes to it all, whether they needed me to install content management systems like WordPress or do front-end web design. Thanks to the time I spent studying programming, I offered Flash programming as well, a capability most agencies didn't have in-house at the time.

I was in demand and making more money than I had as a salaried employee. I thought, "Wow. This is for me."

BLURRED LINES

I was thrilled but I knew I couldn't luxuriate in my early success. You can't go out on your own as a freelancer and expect to relax. Fortunately, I have a strong worth ethic, at least when it comes to business. (Don't ask me to mow the lawn.) Still, I had to be vigilant not to let the rest of my life distract me from my business goals.

HOME LIFE

Blending work and home life was the first challenge. You may recall that popular video that got turned into a meme, where the BBC news correspondent's young daughter bursts into his office on a live newscast, dancing up a storm. That kind of thing happened to me a lot on conference calls with clients. Even if your kids aren't busting down your office door, it's way too easy to get distracted working at home. You think, "Why not throw in a load of laundry or start the dishwasher between meetings?" Don't do it. It will only distract you from what you need to be paying attention to—your business. Staying on task requires discipline.

That said, I had it pretty good. Paula didn't work outside the home, so she was able to take care of the kids most of the time. We did juggle parenting duties a bit—Paula took care of the kids while I worked and I took work breaks to be with the baby—but I got pretty immersed in the work.

Here's how I did it: I'm a night owl by nature, so I often worked until two, three, or four in the morning. The next day, I rolled out of bed, walked down the hallway to my office, and turned on my computer. From that moment on, I was tied to work. If I hadn't eaten and gotten dressed that morning, it wasn't happening. I spent days in boxer shorts, eating only what Paula brought in to me. I was obsessed.

RELIGIOUS LIFE

Meanwhile, I was still attached to my religious community and becoming more conflicted about it by the day. Now that my work schedule was less rigid, I was expected to spend more time in service. That, after all, was why I was *supposed* to be doing all this. When I was employed two years earlier, I dutifully went out in service on the weekends, and was even promoted to ministerial servant.

But now, when I had more time to dedicate to the religion, I was becoming less and less enthusiastic about it, though I couldn't admit it out loud or even to myself. Consciously, I still believed what I'd been taught. I thought maybe Satan was tempting me away from the church with the business. Crazy, I know. But subconsciously, I was bored, and the religion made me feel pressured and guilty instead of fulfilled and happy. Still, I continued to spend some time in the ministry, trying desperately to keep up the facade.

It couldn't last. Deep down, I think I knew it was bullshit. My drive to be involved in the church steadily declined as my business grew.

FIRST CLIENTS: THE GOOD, THE BAD, AND THE CRAZY

And how it grew. Sort of like a garden, where you have to pull a lot of weeds and shovel a lot of shit before you can grow a sustainable crop.

My first client, the property management firm, made it seem easy. The head of the company loved my work turning his amateur websites into polished, professional pages. Every time I turned what was essentially crayon scribbles into a coherent, navigable site, he was over the moon. I wanted more clients like this!

I lucked out for a while. Then came Sean.

Sean came with a fine pedigree—he was a marketing contractor managing an account for one of the top universities in North America. He offered me a prestigious job designing the school's president's report. One of the largest design agencies in the region, called Colour, had been working on it but the school wasn't happy with their work. Why did they choose me? They felt they would have more control over the project working with a freelancer.

It was a red flag that I chose to ignore.

Though my spidey senses were tingling, I charged in. I did have the good sense to quote them an extremely high hourly rate instead of going fixed cost. I'd bill them every month for however many hours it took.

Good thing, too. It took a lot of hours. I had to drive three hours to the university just to present the work. They wanted it in person, printed, and mounted on black mat board. Of course they did.

I got it done and drove up to present it to the university president, Dr. Riley. (He insisted on being called Dr. Riley.) He was Lord Farquaad from Shrek, in the flesh—a tiny little man with the biggest ego on the planet. He would strut around the boardroom yelling at people, terrifying the university staff. He'd shake his head at the work and holler, "No, no, no, that's NO GOOD!" It was what I'd imagine it would be like designing Donald Trump's golden toilet, or something.

I was furious but I was also amused. Clearly, I was meant to be a peon presenting to the king, but all I could think was, "Okay, keep snapping those boards in two and throwing them out the window, doctor. I'm billing for this. I can come back with more and I'll bill you for those, too."

I made a killing on that job. Not that they wanted to pay.

Sometimes, you just have to go to the source. When they stalled on paying the final invoice after they fired me from the project, Kevin opted to just "pop in" to their offices while we were in town. He marched into accounts payable, announced he was there to collect on an overdue invoice, and walked out with a cheque. I felt like my older brother had just kicked the school bully's ass for me.

BUILDING A BIGGER BUSINESS

That summer working for crazy Lord Farquaad sealed it for me—I needed bigger and better clients. To get them, I needed a bigger and better business.

That required a mind shift. I had to stop thinking like a freelancer who works directly for the income. I had to understand that a business is a machine that generates income and revenue. As the business owner, my job was to work on the machine, and let the machine generate income. The gears in the business machine are the departments. One department brings clients in, another manages them and makes them happy, another one executes the work, and another handles operations and finances—and all of the pieces work together.

I struggled to make the shift from worker to owner. I still thought I was supposed to be head designer, account manager, and human resources head. But the more I worked on the business "machine" from the outside, the easier it became.

My experience was fairly typical; it happens across industries. For instance, restaurant chefs often get overwhelmed trying to handle it all. Too often, the chef works crazy hours trying to run every aspect of the restaurant with the same attention to detail she gives to the food. That's a recipe for burnout. Instead, she should create systems and processes to ensure the same high-quality product without requiring her to do everything singlehandedly.

It took me a while to absorb this lesson. When I was running Headspace, I made the same mistake, getting deeply involved in the user experience (UX) engagements and design products. That was the completely wrong way to run that business.

It seemed to work at first—people came to us because they wanted *me* to work on their project—but it wasn't sustainable. They should have been calling us because they wanted to work with our *company*, not me. When I eventually realized this, a light went on. I let it go, and didn't miss the work at all. I should have stepped back sooner.

AIM HIGH

Aim for the moon. Even if you come up short, you still hit an impressively high target. Too many freelancers and entrepreneurs never land a big client, simply because they're aiming too low. Recently, I talked to someone trying to get his web design and marketing business off the ground by taking work from places that paid him incredibly low rates. I wanted to lovingly smack him to wake up from thinking that he couldn't ask for more.

I played the "I could never" game, too. I thought nobody would hire a nineteen-year-old, until they did. Then I thought becoming a freelancer was too big a stretch, until it wasn't. An agency? I could never run an agency! Wrong again. Do you see the pattern here?

If you keep trying, you really can do anything you put your mind to. But you have to have a vision worth targeting. I didn't have a grand vision ten years ago. If I had, I might have gotten to where I am now a lot sooner. Don't aim too low.

MY BROMANCE WITH KEVIN

Both freelancing and entrepreneurship sound like solo endeavours, but they don't have to be lonely occupations. Working with a partner has been a lifesaver for me.

I knew Kevin was an interesting guy as soon as I met him at Modern Media. He told me about how, back home in Maine, he used to run a restaurant and live music venue. One day an inspector came by and told him that, due to regulations, he wasn't allowed to have an outdoor patio. The deck was a huge draw and brought in a lot of revenue during the summer months. So instead of closing the patio down, he just asked to be fined and paid it. The fine was much less than the loss in business would have been. I think the inspector's head may have exploded. Kevin's motto is that if a stupid rule exists, it's always better to ask for forgiveness, rather than seek permission to do it in the first place.

At forty-four, Kevin took his first desk job and sat next to me, a reasonably meek young man. He, on the other hand, started his first business in his twenties, running a popular music club and making tons of cash. Then he moved to Florida and started a coffee company called Manatee Coffee, selling the product online as early as the late nineties. It's in Florida where Kevin met his future wife, Kelly, a nurse from Nova Scotia working abroad. Soon enough, she had him moving up north to her homeland. Kevin told me that he crossed the border with a packed-up U-Haul, under the guise that he was camping for the week. He crossed into Canada as a landed immigrant and years later got his citizenship. Rules? Fuck 'em. After that, he got a job at a marketing agency, though he had no background in advertising. Not a problem.

Kevin broke down boundaries for me. I was nervous to talk about my personal life at work, but Kevin wasn't at all. Not even hot-button issues like religion. In fact, Kevin was very forthcoming with his criticism of religion, even though he knew I was brought up in the Jehovah's Witnesses. We debated religion—he said it was manmade, while I argued for the divine. I was so indoctrinated, I entered these discussions thinking I would convert him. As it turned out, he converted me.

We bonded quickly, and too closely for the comfort of some people we worked for. Our boss, Jaime, walked by one day when I was sitting in Kevin's office chatting. "What is this? Kevin and Kyle Media?" he shot at us with an icy glare. We weren't, but the seeds of our business were planted there. Later, after I had gone out on my own as a freelancer, I thought about forming an agency and knew I wanted Kevin to be my business partner. We were driving in the car together, and I was as nervous as a man getting down on one knee to propose marriage, but I popped this question: "Instead of you doing your own thing and subcontracting it out to me," I asked, "why don't you partner up with me? We'll call it Headspace. We can make it into something."

I was so afraid he'd say no. He didn't.

COMPLEMENTARY STRENGTHS

Merging our worlds was not always easy, just like a real marriage.

The fact was, Kevin and I were different. I just had to realize that was our strength. Put me on design work and I'll give clients what they want every time, but send me on a sales call? No. That was Kevin's territory. I also knew very little about the operational side of business. I didn't know how to set up a corporation or raise working capital. Kevin knew tons.

Like any partnership, we've had our ups and downs—the key to our success is we're never down at the same time. During the ten years of our partnership, when Kevin was dealing with family issues, I stepped in as his support system. At other times, when I was barely keeping it together, he was the strong one. We alternate between those two states. Sure, we've had some arguments along the way, but we're always quick to find common ground, understand the other's viewpoint, and make up.

You can run a business on your own but it's much harder without a cofounder. When things get tough, you won't have anyone to talk to. There's nothing like venting to a business partner.

One of the biggest benefits of having a business partner is that it frees you up to have relationships in the rest of your life that aren't polluted with business. When your spouse isn't an entrepreneur, sharing your worries about missing your year-end revenue goals or needing to fire someone will only bring stress to your relationship. With a business partner to talk to, you can keep your personal life free of that stress.

Some of the biggest agencies in the world have names like Ogilvy & Mather, Saatchi & Saatchi, Weinstein & Kennedy—there's a reason for that.

CHAPTER THREE

THE AGENCY SHIT-SHOW

Our first lesson in our new business: you never know where a project will lead.

One of our first clients at Headspace had a design project for a gourmet pet-treat business called Mucci Pucci (pronounced Moochie Poochie. You know, like Gucci? Eh? Never mind). I designed the website, logo, and packaging, and was quite happy with how it turned out, so I paid to enter it into the local design and advertising awards in Nova Scotia, called the Ice Awards.

With the entry came an event ticket. I couldn't imagine going myself; all those agency staffers adorned with soul patches, wearing T-shirts and jeans with blazers, puffing their chests and patting themselves on the back. It would wear me out. I really didn't want to go. Fortunately, Kevin—aka Captain Schmooze—did, so I told him to take the ticket and drum up some work while he was there.

And just like that, Kevin reconnected with an agency where he used to work—one of the biggest ad agencies in town. Just by talking to people at the event, he landed our first real client, one that ended up bringing us tons of development work. To top off the evening, Kevin called me that night to tell me I'd won the award for design packaging with Mucci Pucci. What a night! Our little agency that could was starting to build some buzz in the local community.

Connections like these were enough for us at first. In fact, we were hesitant to grow too fast or too big. We had seen too many other agencies flounder under the weight of their monthly expenses. Our solution: hire independent contractors. They only get paid when you get paid. It worked for a while but the freelancers we hired were not always reliable, and we had deadlines to meet. Hiring contractors was also more expensive than we expected, and it was eating into our profit margin. On a $10,000 project, we might clear a whopping $1,000 after all of the contractors were paid.

Maybe we were charging too little. We were probably

spending too little—we were nervous about even renting office space, let alone hiring employees. Our mindset was that we should keep expenses extremely low to improve our profit. Over time, we realized this approach was shortsighted and decided to hire a versatile employee who could do a variety of tasks—a little bit of design along with programming, which we especially needed. That person was Ricky, our first employee.

HIRING HITS AND MISSES

I'd known Ricky for a few years. When we first met, his then-wife was studying to become a Jehovah's Witness, and the older couple she was studying with invited me to a barbecue to "encourage" the couple—in other words, form a personal connection that makes it possible to socially pressure the non-Witnesses into becoming baptized members. More on that in chapter 5.

Ricky and I are both guitar players, and were both into web design, so we hit it off right away. I knew he was underemployed, working at a rinky-dink agency that did shoddy work, a "websites while you wait" style of company. We loved talking shop at the Kingdom Hall, and I saw him as a diamond in the rough, so I invited him to join the company. I tried to bring him on as a freelancer but, like many people, he balked, insisting on a full-time, salaried position. We gave it to him because we knew he was a sponge for knowledge. He soaks up everything and learns rapidly. When he came to us he didn't know anything about CSS (Cascading Style Sheets, the web language for making HTML look good), but two weeks later, he was better at it than I was.

Even though I'd never had an employee before, it wasn't difficult at all to add Ricky to the business, because he did such good work and I could bring problems to him to solve. His programming and technical skills were much better than his design skills, so I coached him and mentored him as we grew, until he became a strong designer, too.

Ricky and I are best friends—he was there with me throughout my transition out of the Jehovah's Witnesses, and he and Kevin were both best men at my recent wedding. Ricky has also been good for the business. I have endless trust in him in his current role as chief product officer, where he leads the product department, who design features and improvements to Proposify.

ROOKIE MISTAKE

It must have been beginner's luck. Our next hire was a different story.

We knew we needed a back-end programmer who could

handle the server side and database programming—someone to manage the engineering piece while we worked on front-end website development. Being the creative thinkers we are, we came up with the perfect solution—we'd hire a college intern! They need experience, they're cheap, and they'd be just as good as anybody else! Brilliant! Off I went to my community college to recruit a student to come in for an internship.

On his first day, I knew I had made a rookie mistake. When I showed him what we were doing and invited him to jump in and solve some problems, he looked like nothing more than a frightened turtle. He was not prepared for what I was asking him to do. The next day, I got an email from him saying, "I don't think this line of work is for me. I don't think I'm going to come in." While causing a fresh college grad to give up his career path after one day of working at my company isn't at the top of my list of achievements, it is there.

Clearly, we had to look for someone with more experience.

NOT TAKING CARE OF BUSINESS

Armed with our new knowledge, did we launch a robust search process? No, we did not. We hired the first developer who came in for an interview.

Raymond looked great on paper and seemed to be a nice, personable guy. Good enough. (We didn't check any references. We didn't vet him in any way.)

We started Raymond with one project to ease him in, a tourism website. His job was to make it possible to input latitude and longitude coordinates into a content management system and have the locations appear in Google Maps. Simple enough. He worked on this project, and only this project, for two or three weeks, yet he couldn't seem to finish. The rest of the website was ready to deliver, and the client was champing at the bit. We stalled, and went back to Raymond. He told us it wasn't ready.

Something was up with this guy. I got so frustrated that I went into the office one Saturday, determined to figure out what was going on. With one quick search I found an online tutorial, and with two hours of coding, I'd completed the project and delivered it to the client.

I don't know what Raymond was doing all those weeks. Looking at websites or watching YouTube? Whatever the case, he had to go.

That was the first time I'd ever fired someone. It was tough but paying somebody for three weeks to do nothing was worse. Every dollar was precious in those first few months, and I felt like we'd already wasted lots of money.

THIRD TIME'S THE CHARM

After the Raymond debacle, I was at my wits' end. Then I remembered Nick, the technology director who had set up my computer for me when I interned at Impact. I had liked him from the beginning. Remember the Ent character of Treebeard in *The Lord of the Rings*? A wise, ancient, half-man, half-tree with a deep booming voice who loved nature and poetry? Nick was kind of like that guy. He once lived in the mountains of British Columbia as a tree surveyor. He had a full beard and loved to talk about vinyl, wine, and, coincidentally, *The Lord of the Rings*. He was the agency's only developer for a long time, and he taught me a lot about code and technology.

Over a few coffees, text messages, and phone calls, I tried to convince him to come work for us. He'd been at Impact for close to ten years, but I managed to win him over. Nick became our third hire and a successful one. He stayed with us for as long as I was with the company.

LESSONS LEARNED

After adding Nick, we thought we were done hiring. We certainly didn't see the need to hire an accountant, or a finance officer, or an operations head. We assumed more employees just meant more management issues and more expense.

As you can see, we were reluctant to increase our overhead. The only employees we felt comfortable hiring were designers and developers, who could generate revenue for the business. We thought that any new hires had to do billable work. That was another rookie mistake. You can't skimp on people; you need people to grow your company.

Running a business is a bit like being a movie director—Quentin Tarantino doesn't need to know how to do cinematography, costume design, or post production. His job is to have the vision for the movie and articulate that vision to other talented professionals he hires.

When you're starting out, you usually wear all the hats. You're the film student holding the camera and lights and saying "action." But as you grow, you have to hire, recruit, and retain really good talent. Your job is to find the right people with the necessary skills to help you grow the business.

Despite our reluctance to hire a non-billable employee, we eventually had enough clients that we needed an account manager to keep clients happy and their projects on track. We hired someone with experience and talent, Amy, who came in and hit the ground running.

CLIENT CRAZINESS

Once our internal house was in order—even though we were still meeting in a section of town where it wasn't unusual to see a pantless guy walking down the street at lunchtime—we needed clients. Any clients, really. As with hiring, we were not nearly picky enough at first.

The crux of the problem was that we had no real point of differentiation. We didn't know what value our company brought to the world. We knew people needed websites. We made websites. What more was there to say? (To give you an idea of our level of sophistication, the tagline on our home page was literally "We design awesome websites." That was our entire value proposition.)

DR. BALLS

It won't come as a surprise that we took on any client who came in the door. One early pick was so memorable—in the worst way—that years later I asked Amy to write an article for the Proposify blog about him. We called him "Dr. Balls."

Dr. Balls billed himself as a pretty big deal in technology; he said he was in the running to lead eHarmony but ultimately didn't make the cut. His business card listed a number of degrees, letters, and initials after his name. Before Amy met him, she had high expectations. She pictured him as a Sherlock Holmes-type with a clay pipe and a houndstooth jacket—not a dirty Raiders coat and the smell of mouse droppings. She could only hope maybe he was an eccentric genius.

The meeting was set for ten in the morning and he showed up at nine—on purpose. We had no waiting room or lounge, so he just sat there with us all working nearby, feeling under his scrutiny. At ten, we ushered the good doctor into the meeting room to discuss his big idea for a social app. It seemed harmless enough—he wanted to offer a personality test that would match users with friends or dates—until he started saying words like "five-star hotties" and "porno button."

We knew right then we should say no, but he was fine with our budget and we needed the money. So, we moved on to design. As professionally as I could, I asked him what the "porno button" was for. His response: "You know: *enter here*."

Unbelievably, the conversation devolved from there. The most critical part of the site, he told us, would be his "gyrating balls." (Thus his nickname.) He meant Venn diagrams, to illustrate how well somebody was matched with someone else, but that's not what he said. At this point, I had to excuse myself from the room. I've got to hand it to myself, really—I didn't crack a smile while I was at the table.

We designed it all just the way he wanted. The site was a piece of garbage but we exchanged services since his son was a developer. Balls Junior built our early prototype of Proposify, a barely functioning demo I used to pitch at DemoCamp, a local startup event that helped us secure our early stage funding. Eventually, the matchmaking app project fizzled. As Amy wrote on her blog post, Dr. Balls had to take his twirling gonads elsewhere. I'm pretty sure why he wasn't a fit for eHarmony.

COLOUR BLINDNESS

We hoped Dr. Balls was an outlier, but we quickly realized any client interaction can go south, even a seemingly straightforward project with the professional staff of Nova Scotia's Department of Agriculture. We were hired to design a fairly simple website. There were no red flags in sight, and yet the woman we worked with at the department made it impossible to do a good job. It was like she *wanted* the site to look bad.

After presenting what we thought were solid options for a well-designed website that met her needs, she wasn't happy. We tried again. She was still not happy. This happened over and over again until we ran out of ideas. Finally, I told Ricky to make the ugliest website he could make. It was disgusting. She loved it.

There was one more thing, though. (Of course there was.) She kept pushing back on the colour. Because the Nova Scotian flag is blue, she was keen to get the same exact blue colour on her site, and our blue wasn't doing it for her. We sampled the exact hex codes to make sure it matched precisely. No go. We tried lighter, we tried darker, we tried different shades. It was always wrong. She said she would send us what she wanted. We didn't know what she meant, until one day a postcard arrived in the mail. It was a card with a purple kangaroo on it. On the back, she had written, "This is the kind of blue I'm looking for." Lesson: colour-blind clients probably shouldn't pick their website colours.

COMING INTO FOCUS

We were getting pretty burned out by these kinds of clients. Fortunately, there were some gems as well, like Jamie Vander Kooi (pronounced "Koo," so I naturally renamed him The Goo, and variations such as Goo-Man and Goo-Man-Chu), who worked for Prince Edward Island tourism. He ended up being one of our most profitable contacts. The connection was invaluable, because it's incredibly hard to break into large enterprises and government departments without a champion on the inside selling you to the decision makers. Jamie recommended us to every government department he could.

At the same time, we started attracting bigger clients.

When we went from building $5,000 websites to a $120,000 university project, we were elated. It seemed like such a huge amount. Unfortunately, it turned out the project itself was even more massive, and a nightmare to manage.

We were still taking any job we could, but as I looked around, I noticed other companies that specialized in certain industries. VERB, a local competitor, focused only on travel and tourism. They didn't just "do websites," they helped travel brands increase bookings. That was smart. VERB became known as the best in their field, and landed accounts with Royal Caribbean and big US golf courses. They grew to an agency with over one hundred employees and millions of dollars in revenue. We didn't do that, and that's why we stayed small and struggled.[6]

Our "say yes to everything" approach only compounded our lack of profitability. We had to learn it was beneficial to say no sometimes. In fact, if we were able to say no more often than yes, that was a good sign. When we started specializing, we began to grow. But that wouldn't happen until our next business.

I learned a lot over the five years I ran a marketing agency,

---

[6] Kevin and I earned a steady paycheque for most of the lifecycle of Headspace, each taking home about $70,000/year, but we got into a fair bit of debt and never achieved any true long-term wealth for the amount of work and stress it was to run the agency.

and I want to leave a few takeaways for anyone running an agency or considering starting one:

- **Service businesses can be lucrative businesses for the founders.** Unlike software startups, where you may raise money and lose control to investors, agencies are usually owned completely by the principals and can generate strong cash flow. While the gross margins are lower, as are the multiples in the event of an acquisition, the company is 100 percent yours, and that's worth something. It's wise to reinvest profit to fuel growth, but also take some of that cash and invest into long-term investments that yield compound interest. A good year can turn into a bad year at the drop of a hat, so make hay while the sun shines and don't waste your cash on buying too many shiny things.
- **There are a lot of downsides to running an agency.** Clients are demanding and can be difficult to please, and it's your job as a service business to, well, service them, and keep them happy. Every business is a grind, but agencies are in a category unto themselves. Projects go over budget. Clients stop paying their bills. Employees hop around to different agencies and leave you. Service businesses require people to scale, and so the only way to truly become a multimillionaire from your agency is to get comfortable with hiring a lot of employees, creating a sales engine that can consis-

tently drive new business, and building the systems and processes needed to scale.

- **Don't make the same mistakes I did.** I know plenty of entrepreneurs, several of whom I call friends, who run great service businesses and live comfortable lifestyles. In almost every case it's because they picked a specialty or niche that they can be among the best in their field at. Go narrow and deep. Take on only high-paying clients that fit your ideal profile or target persona. Sell ongoing monthly retainers that generate steady, sustainable cash flow. The transition from a freelance business to a profitable, scaling agency requires a completely different mindset. If you think of it as just hiring junior support staff, you're going to run into trouble. You need to hire great talent and let them build the business for you. Build a well-oiled machine that can operate without you.

In the next section, I'll talk about my two years of personal hell, the end of our agency, and how we gave Proposify a fighting chance.

PART II
ARMAGEDDON

CHAPTER FOUR
—

TINKERING WITH PRODUCTS

If you're an elder millennial like myself (or older), chances are you've probably played Tetris before. At first, the coloured blocks aren't a problem to manage, and you can match the patterns pretty easily, clearing them out of your way. Eventually, you make a couple of mistakes and you have a large pillar of blocks on one side of the screen, which creates less and less room for error. By the end of the round, your entire screen is filled with blocks and one wrong move means game over.

It's kind of like that running a business. I've shared a lot of my mistakes building my first company—mistakes many first-time agency owners make. And really, making mistakes is a part of learning and getting better. Still, when you make too many mistakes, they pile up. Eventually, you're in so deep there's not much you can do to save yourself, except tread water and try not to drown. We treaded water for a long time. On a good week, we'd have money to deposit in the company bank account on Monday so people could get paid on Thursday. Other times, we had no idea where that money would come from. Sometimes the only way to make payroll was for Kevin to lend his personal savings to the business.

It wasn't that we lacked receivables, but sometimes we couldn't wait even one extra day for that payment. Several times, when a payment was just a couple days past due, Kevin pretended to have a meeting in the client's hometown so he could offer to "swing by" and pick up the cheque, saving them the postage. It worked. We did whatever it took to stay afloat.

Our cash flow roller coaster took us on a wild ride. Projects went over budget because the client made changes we hadn't anticipated. When that happened, we would draw on our line of credit to pull us out of the dip. Then the next project would take twice as long as we'd planned, eating up our fixed fee too quickly. So, we'd borrow more money. Not a great idea. Headspace maxed out at $150,000 in loans very quickly.

SEEKING STABILITY

We knew we needed to get out of the agency business and into SaaS and selling subscriptions. We were inspired by Basecamp's origin story—how Jason Fried and David Heinemeier Hansson ran a web design business before offering Basecamp as project management software. Eventually, their subscription business took over and became more profitable than the agency business. That sounded like a pretty smooth transition. Surely, we could do the same.

We started investing my time, and the time of our employees who weren't busy, into product development. I'll tell you about each SaaS product we tried before deciding to focus on Proposify:

1. **Site Tea.** We had found that, perhaps due to our lack of strong positioning in the market as a premium web shop, we had to turn down a lot of mom-and-pop leads who simply didn't have the budget to work with us. But what if there was a way for us to generate a templated website for them that they could customize themselves, allow them to pay a small monthly subscription, say twenty dollars a month, and we would include the hosting? Sounds familiar, right? We created a minimum viable product, using WordPress, and we called the product Site Tea.[7] We

---

7   We called it Site Tea because picking a template was kind of like selecting a flavour of tea. Years later, we would use a coffee motif for Proposify. Apparently I have an affinity for hot beverages.

got a few subscribers, but ultimately the product was garbage compared to the newly emerging Wix and Squarespace, and we didn't have the wherewithal to double down and focus on the DIY website market.

2. **Social Gopher.** Next, we built social media analytics software, called Social Gopher. Social media was just beginning to blossom at this time and our clients were starting to talk about it.[8] We were already producing a social media monitoring report that we used to sell our services. Why not make it into a SaaS product? We could have an app generate the report automatically—just crawl websites and compile it all together. What could go wrong? A lot, as it turned out. We got two or three customers paying one hundred dollars a month, but we clearly needed more. Too late, we discovered we couldn't handle more, because there were crawling limits we had never heard of. We heard soon enough, when we began to exceed the number of requests allowed to the websites' API. Twitter just shut us off after ten clients. We could have paid a third-party provider to handle all the requests and send them back to us, but it would have cost thousands of dollars a month. We were struggling to make payroll. Social Gopher was quickly shut down.

3. **Extrify.** We had already built a custom extranet for a client in Alberta, a recycling and wastewater

---

[8] Radian6, an Atlantic Canadian social monitoring SaaS company, had recently sold to Salesforce for $326 million.

management facility, to handle their internal communications. We owned the IP and there was nothing about the product that was inherent to wastewater; it had features like messages, file uploads, group permissions, chat, scheduling, and so on. There are a lot of large businesses that need a product like this, and Microsoft SharePoint is the industry standard. Like most enterprise software incumbents, SharePoint is ugly, hard to use, and everyone hates it. So, we packaged it up and sold it to another handful of subscribers. Extrify wasn't a colossal failure; it did end up being a selling point later when we sold the agency business—as part of the deal, the buyers got to keep Extrify (but not Proposify). I was more passionate about my proposal software concept and it was difficult to spread my focus across so many different projects.

Most entrepreneurs need to swing and miss a few times before they hit a home run, and with every business you make mistakes and try not to repeat them the next time. The upside of building all of these SaaS products was that we were learning a lot. The first three attempts at SaaS many not have been successful, but we were getting experienced at building SaaS.

As many mistakes as we made with SaaS, we made even more when it came to running an agency. I touched on some of them in the last chapter. Here are some core lessons I learned running Headspace.

CHARGE A PREMIUM

Our first, and perhaps most painful, lesson was financial. We had to get the message that it wasn't worth charging a low fee just to keep a lead from walking away. Eventually, we got it. We came to see that charging a premium and moving up-market was important for longevity. We needed to be more of a premium agency that works with Fortune 5000 companies who have six- and seven-figure marketing budgets. We never quite got there, but we could have in time.

Avoid wasting your time with small deals where the client still quibbles over price. If there is to be any quibbling, you need to be sure you have the upper hand. No more throwing out a budget number the client is only too eager to snap up. I got into the habit of starting the money conversation by asking the client to tell me *their* budget. Or, I might throw out a high number, but not my highest number.

These techniques worked so much better, I wish I had understood them much, much earlier. I could have used them when we booked the university project. Instead, we threw out the biggest number we could imagine—$150,000—way too little for what they wanted us to accomplish. If I had known what I know now, I probably could have asked for, and received, half a million dollars.

I would relearn this lesson later with Proposify. In the early days of running a SaaS business, it's easier to sell to consumers or small businesses at a low monthly fee, like nineteen dollars a month. But as you scale, those small businesses cancel their subscription at a much higher rate, which impacts your growth, lifetime value, business valuation, and a number of other important metrics. Moving up-market and selling to larger businesses and enterprise is a common way for SaaS companies to grow because big businesses pay you more and they rarely churn once they've adopted your software. Charging too little, out of fear of losing the sale, is a mistake entrepreneurs constantly make, and one you need discipline to avoid.

HOW TO CREATE STEADY CASH FLOW

Making a big ask can definitely work in your favour. Then your only problem is actually getting paid, which can be harder than you might think.

In the beginning when we sold $10,000 websites, we typically asked for $2,000 up front, then started working. It might be weeks or months before we could present something to the client. It often took longer to get any feedback from them. Sometimes clients just vanished. Or they would return after a long, unexplained absence. In our naïveté, we just picked up where they had left off and didn't charge for the delay. It could be a long haul before we saw the entire $10,000.

Projects got delayed for the most ridiculous reasons. I'll never forget the commercial real estate company owner who wanted social media buttons at the bottom of his site, but refused to set up the accounts behind the buttons. Fine. We'd launch without the buttons. The launch went well, but we noticed he wasn't paying his final invoice. You can guess why not—the original design specified social media buttons, and they weren't on the final website. No matter that it was his own fault. I wanted to reach through the phone and throttle him. In the end, I changed his password to the website back end and locked him out until he paid.

One of the reasons Proposify has succeeded is that we don't have to do this kind of negotiation over and over again. With the subscription model, recurring revenue not only brings in fees on a consistent basis, it compounds our results every month. There hasn't been a time since we hit product/market fit when we've generated less monthly recurring revenue (MRR) than the previous month. Now, sometimes we want it to go up higher and faster, but it never goes down and it rarely stays the same.

Never worrying about having enough cash to pay myself or my employees is a gift I try to never take for granted.

HOW TO PROTECT YOURSELF

Another crucial lesson we learned in the early years: always have a contract that specifies the scope of the work. One university client, for example, had unreasonable expectations; they wanted us to create their course materials. Because that wasn't communicated in the contract, we misunderstood. We thought *they* were providing the content and we were building the software. Not that anyone said as much in any conversation, or noted it in the budget. Still, they wanted to hold us accountable, because in their head, they assumed we would know they needed us to build their course material, despite the fact that they were the psychology researchers—not us! We did what we could to accommodate their request, but in hindsight we should have just said no and hired a lawyer if things got hostile. As it was, we worked on this project for over a year and got paid upfront, but with no end in sight.

Having our lawyer deal with their legal team on the contract would have protected us, but we were too desperate to close the deal and cash the cheque. (We signed a contract, but the client had their legal team write it and we were too cheap to hire our own lawyer to review it.)

In Nova Scotia, many deals are sealed with a handshake and, early on, that seemed just fine to us. We learned quickly that it wasn't. One such "good old boy" engaged us this way, and we did an upfront discovery even though he hadn't signed the contract or paid the invoice. We had idle people who we wanted to get busy, so we got rolling. When we had sunk about ten hours into the project, the client changed his mind and pulled out of the deal, and we never got paid a cent.

Never start a project without a signed contract. Get it in writing, and if your client makes amendments, hire a good attorney on retainer to review it. Never talk to your client's lawyer. Only lawyers talk to lawyers.

DON'T BE A COG IN THE MACHINE; BUILD THE MACHINE

One of the hardest lessons for me to learn was that, as a founder and entrepreneur, you have to work *on* the business, not *in* it. I had heard that advice when I was running Headspace, but I didn't know how to apply it. What did it mean to work on the business?

It meant taking a different perspective, coming out of the trenches and looking at the whole picture. That's not always easy for someone used to doing it all himself. For instance, at Headspace, I was so caught up in the day-to-day logistics, I failed to pay attention to any of the key performance indicators to manage profitability. Instead, I was still working with clients and sitting in on discovery meetings, or installing WordPress plugins, when those were no longer my jobs. My job, as founder, was to bring in new clients and oversee operations. I didn't have time to spend in the guts of the machine. I should have breezed into those discovery meetings, shaken a few hands, and then gone back to recruiting new clients.

Since building Proposify, Kevin and I have a new goal: to hire ourselves out of our jobs. Not because we're lazy (okay, we're a little lazy), but because it's the responsible thing to do: create a scalable business that can be sold. Less than a year ago, Kevin was overwhelmed with human resources and office management. I had to convince him to hire employees to do it all. Now he doesn't know what he would do without Jennie and Cavell, who are running HR and office management, respectively.

An agency is made up of a handful of departments. Your job is to recruit heads to run these departments and hold them accountable for hitting business metrics, like sales revenue and billable hours. In an agency or consulting business, your departments look like this:

- **Business development.** These are the people who craft relationships, hop on planes, and participate in pitching new business. The movers and shakers. The

salespeople. This is the hardest job to outsource as an agency founder, and thus the last department you'll build.
- **Client services.** This is your customer success department, made up of account managers. They communicate with clients, make them happy, and reach out to earn repeat business.
- **Production.** Depending on the type of service business you run, these are the folks who make the donuts. The designers, producers, strategists, marketing consultants, and developers. Their job is to deliver top-quality work that gets clients results.
- **Operations.** Don't skimp on this. You need bean counters who make sure clients are being billed, projects aren't over budget, financial metrics are being hit, and the business is running smoothly.
- **Human resources.** Recruiting and onboarding new talent, handling the day-to-day management of employees, like performance reviews and firing, managing payroll and health benefits, and deciding whether your office needs a foosball table for "culture."

That's pretty much it. If you can build these departments and employ a few good men and women to lead them, you just might have a profitable agency on your hands, with at least 20 to 30 percent gross margins. As a business owner, you should be thinking about how to make the business run so that you never *have to* be there. If you ever have to sell the business, it will be that much more valuable to the new owners. If the business depends on your name and sales ability to keep going, it's worth a lot less to a potential buyer. You need to be able to just hand over the keys. A potential buyer would immediately know that the business won't survive without you, and that they'll have to hire a whole new team to make up for losing you.

HOW TO STAY MOTIVATED

You might wonder what kept us going through all of our challenges. I don't know how it is for others, but for me, the more difficult the terrain, the harder I push. It might just be the way I'm wired—facing problems makes me excited to get out of bed. When things seem easy, I actually feel more worried—worried that I might become complacent.

A couple of years after Proposify started growing, I felt like I was getting a little too relaxed. The business was growing and everyone was happy. That was great, but I was uneasy, because there were no problems to solve. I needed a problem. It wasn't long before I got one.

When we brought investors on board in 2018, Kevin and I set the ambitious goal of reaching $10 million in annual revenue by the end of the year. Our investors were expecting us to hit that goal, and we hit challenges along the way. I'm actually more excited about the business than I was last year, because I've got a high benchmark to reach, and the pressure of a new board. Now I'm working even harder than I was a year ago, and getting coached to improve my performance as a CEO. I'm in that startup mindset again. Fear works for me.

Spite works pretty well, too. I was very motivated to prove wrong all the people who said I'd never make it on my own in business. Someone will always doubt you. Even when we were successfully running Proposify, people kept telling us it wouldn't last. Everyone, from clients to investors, had their opinions. Kevin and I had to turn that around and say, "Oh really? You think we'll fail? Watch us prove you wrong!" Some might say we have a chip on our shoulder. Maybe, but we've earned the chip. Entrepreneurs tend to be arrogant people because they have to be; on some level you need to believe you're right and everyone else is wrong because otherwise you'll give up before you start. Naturally, that arrogance has to be tempered with the humility to learn from your mistakes and adjust course as needed.

PERFECTION IS THE ENEMY OF DONE

To be successful, you have to walk the line between careful and reckless. Starting out, it's better to perform customer research so you don't end up working on a problem nobody has. We were apt to approach each product with enthusiasm, but we seldom validated the product ahead of time. Instead, each time we got an idea in our heads, like Social Gopher, Extrify, or Site Tea, we jumped into the fun part—building version one—without doing any research. We tried to build the full vision for what the product should be instead of just building a small part, a minimum viable product, and showing it to potential customers to understand where we needed to go next.

Even when we started Proposify, we didn't validate it. Thankfully, our intuition was right. We could have been earlier to market with it, but instead treated it more like a side project, letting short-term client projects take priority over the one that would sustain us long term. We should have dedicated one employee's time to Proposify and kept them off client projects—that's what Basecamp did. Eventually, we got on a grant program and hired Jonathan to work on Proposify day in and day out.

Once you've got someone dedicated to product development, you face a new question: When to launch? Here's your answer: go home and launch it. That's my best advice. No matter what shape it's in, put it out there and start seeing what people think. It can have bugs, because guess what? It will always have bugs, from the day you ship it to the day you sell it. The longer you wait to launch, the longer you wait to learn. There's a caveat here: if you're already a well-established company with an existing customer base, you'll need to tread more lightly. You don't want to piss off or disappoint your customers by releasing an unstable product. But if you're starting out and relatively unknown, or selling to a completely new market, you can afford to look the fool for a little while. It's the cost of learning.

Perfectionism holds people back. Some of them are afraid of what people will say; nobody wants to be told their baby is ugly, but that might be just what you need to hear. If you don't hear those messages, you'll never know what you need to improve.

HOW TO THRIVE BEYOND LAUNCH

So you've created the "perfect" product, and launch day is here. Launch day gets good press; you'd think it was all cheers, customers, and steady growth from that day forward. More often, launch day comes and goes, and nothing much happens at all. You don't hear cheers, just crickets. Or you get a few clients, but they try the product and don't like it. Or they sign up to a paid account and then leave.

Most people don't realize that the launch is only one step. After that comes months and months of iterating, learning, and trying to figure out what's going to resonate and net you the ever-elusive product/market fit. You have to pick up the phone and talk to your customers every day. You have to make the time, be patient, and keep your interest high in the face of many unknowns. In the words of Steve Perry, from the band Journey, don't stop believing.

Fortunately, most entrepreneurs don't mind stepping out into the unknown. They're the ones eager to jump out of the plane with no parachute, figuring out on the way down how they can build a plane. You just have to take that first step.

Eventually, we decided to sell our agency and raise a small amount of money to give Proposify the shot it needed to fly. I'll share that story in a later chapter, but first, I want you to know what was going on in my personal life that changed everything about who I was.

CHAPTER FIVE

THE LORD TAKETH

Running Headspace was one of the hardest things I've ever done, but at the same time, it saved me. Work provided a distraction from my crumbling personal life. Other than in my relationship with my young son, Micah, I was miserable. I was miserable in my marriage, I was miserable being stuck in a religion I had doubts about, and I was miserable about feeling that way. As difficult as the business was, I was glad to bury myself in it and escape the rest of my life.

I had so much to run away from. You've probably heard the story of Job, from the Bible. He was kind of like God's guinea pig. Attempting to win a bet with Satan, God allowed Job to lose his wealth, his livestock, his health, his reputation, and his family. I could relate. For at least a year, I felt like I was the modern Job.

COLLAPSE AT HOME

My trials really started to add up in 2009, the first year of Headspace, with my separation from Paula. The separation was painful, but necessary, because life at home had become too chaotic for me, my stepdaughter, and one-year-old Micah. Paula was in a downward spiral. Addicted to prescription sleeping pills, she was either lying in bed all day or out forging cheques in my name. Her behaviour became more erratic and unpredictable, and she eventually tried to take a whole bottle of pills.

Completely overwhelmed, I moved out and got a small apartment close to work, a move that made total sense, but didn't last. The Jehovah's Witnesses belief system doesn't allow for divorce except in cases of adultery. Even though our household was unhealthy, we succumbed to the pressure to stay together, and by next winter, we were living together again, though not much had changed. I was stuck.

DEALING WITH LOSS

The one saving grace in this period was that Micah and I spent every weekend with my parents. I didn't realize at first how precious those days were; I was just glad to spend time with my parents, who were essentially my only friends. Only too soon, I found out our days together would be shorter than I ever expected, when my dad was diagnosed with hepatitis C and liver disease.

Apparently, he'd lived with it his whole life without realizing it, but now it was serious, though I didn't understand that right away. The doctors didn't talk about the disease in terms of months or years to live—they actually made it seem like liver disease could go on a long time—so I tried to put it out of my mind.

The Jehovah's Witnesses and my role in the church continued to occupy my thoughts. I was becoming disengaged, skipping most meetings. I had stopped studying, praying, and going out in the door-to-door preaching work. I wasn't openly questioning the religion yet, but I was headed in that direction, and the church community may have known it. They put a lot of pressure on me to fall back in line, telling me I was weak in my faith and needed to return to the fold. I was even told by my mother, "You need to think about those kids"—Witnesses believe that when Armageddon comes, God will not only execute nonbelievers, but their children also. I was starting to feel as if I were being manipulated. It was the church community itself that had asked me to step down from my ministerial servant post when Paula and I split up. It was they who decreed that I couldn't be a pillar of the community while I was having marital difficulties. Now they wanted me to immerse myself in the church again, and I resisted.

In 2011, my dad's health went downhill quickly. He

started to lose a lot of weight and his stomach bloated with fluids that had to be drained. He started to look like a cancer patient. When we celebrated my parents' thirty-fifth wedding anniversary—a wedding anniversary is pretty much the only thing you can celebrate as a Jehovah's Witness—he was very sick. He slept a lot and got up only occasionally.

Seeing him lying there, I felt like one more pillar of my life was slipping away. It was especially unsettling because my dad had always been a strong, though sometimes polarizing, presence. He was the guy who said what he meant and meant what he said. In those last few days, however, he seemed childlike. My dad had become more affectionate as he got older, but I always felt embarrassed being kissed on the cheek by another grown man. As his last hours passed by, I kissed his forehead like he was a newborn baby.

On January 20, 2012, I watched my father die. His last day felt endless, and it marked a turning point in my relationship with the church. I couldn't accept the comfort offered by people from the Kingdom Hall, because their words suddenly sounded like nonsense to me. My father was only sleeping, they said. He'll be back, they said. I didn't buy it. I knew he was gone, not just sleeping until he'd wake up again in paradise.

The religion's reassurances rang hollow that day, and at

my father's funeral. Like all Jehovah's Witness funerals, the service wasn't so much centred on celebrating the life of the person as it was concerned with recruiting any non-JW friends and relatives who might attend. Predictably, the service ended with a call to action for newcomers to sign up for a personal home Bible study. That's right, my dad's funeral was a fucking sales pitch.

It was time to leave the church. I'd known it for a long time, but the indoctrination was powerful. Put simply, I was afraid. I'd heard all my life about the coming Armageddon, and that the only way I could avoid dying (and my kids dying) was to be strong in the faith. I thought, if that's the way God is going to handle it, I don't want to worship that kind of God. I was close to being done.

"NAPKIN" SKETCH

For a long time after my father died, I just felt numb. I wasn't emotionally present for the birth of my son Ty a month later, at least not the way I had been with Micah. I felt guilty about that, but I was simply depleted.

Fortunately, Kevin and I had planned a trip to London, UK, which helped me emerge from the darkness. Travelling so far was exciting for me—it was the first time that I'd ever left North America—and it inspired me to start thinking creatively about the future.

On the plane ride over, I was reading Steve Jobs's official biography, and I reflected on how I could make a dent in the universe by creating something that didn't yet exist. Proposify was that thing, and it was beginning to take shape in my mind. I began to take notes during our flight home on the only paper at hand, the airplane barf bag. I sketched it all out and handed it to Kevin. He loved it, and told me to save the barf bag so we could remember this moment when Proposify hit the big time. (I wish I had listened. The barf bag remains lost to the annals of history.)

A BELIEF SYSTEM CRUMBLES

Though I was eager to start a new chapter when I returned home, my thinking was still hazy, particularly around religion. In some ways, I still believed in God and the religion I'd grown up in; it was all I'd ever known. In other ways, I didn't *really* believe, not deep down. I felt terribly guilty about my disbelief, and my inability to resolve the inner struggle was giving me cognitive dissonance. I was having panic attacks and trouble sleeping.

As I lay awake one night, I started considering reading what people who had left the Jehovah's Witnesses had to say—people called "apostates" by the Watchtower. With trepidation I typed "Jehovah's Witnesses" into a Google search and skipped past the official website, jw.org. Reading a website or book might not seem like a big deal, but in the religion, reading apostate literature is strictly forbidden. People who have left the church are painted as deserters, traitors, and liars. They are Satan's minions, to be feared and avoided at all costs. Fear and hatred of apostates was ingrained in me at a young age; I'd been told never to listen to an apostate because they are "mentally diseased" and their words are like poison. But here I was doing just that.

I was terrified of the consequences, but I knew I couldn't continue living with the conflict going on in my head. I kept reading. My rationale? The truth can stand up to scrutiny, so if the church's message really was true, the apostates' stories would be nothing but lies, and I'd see right through them. I had nothing to lose by reading. As I began to read websites like jwfacts.com, I was shocked at what I learned. I dug deeper and read a PDF version of *Crisis of Conscience* by Raymond Franz, a former member of the Governing Body.[9]

The irony was, it wasn't so much the words of the "apostates" that swayed me; simply reading the organization's old literature convinced me I was in a cult. As I read quotes from old *Watchtower* and *Awake* magazines, I realized

---

9   The Governing Body is a small group of men who live at Watchtower headquarters in New York. They are venerated, much like the pope is in Catholicism, and considered by Witnesses to be the sole channel through which God communicates to his people. That a member of the Governing Body left and was banished from the religion is remarkable, and has only ever happened once, in the case of Franz.

they were constantly predicting the end of the world, and it never happened. Nobody called them on it, because the older issues went out of circulation or got whitewashed later on. Most Witnesses never saw the evidence that the governing body was misleading them. We had been reminded at nearly every meeting since I could remember that the "end is just around the corner" and that we are living in the last days. As it turns out, Watchtower had been preaching that the end was nigh as far back as the nineteenth century, giving out specific dates for the end, including 1914, 1925, and 1975, and yet here we still are. Instead of issuing a statement after each prediction came and went without fiery judgement, they instead played it off as though they had never predicted it, and it was the individual witnesses' fault for misunderstanding their words and building up too much expectation.

I dug more and found information about decades of child abuse cover-ups in the religion. More pieces fell into place. I remembered years ago, as a ministerial servant, being taken into a backroom by an elder in my Kingdom Hall. The church headquarters sent out a directive to elders asking every man serving in a leadership role[10] if we'd ever sexually abused a child. It was an extremely uncomfortable question to be asked, and

---

10 In the Jehovah's Witnesses, women are not allowed to serve in any leadership or teaching capacity. They are allowed to preach to the outside public, but not allowed to give talks to the congregation unless it's a demonstration or in the case of no baptized male being present, they must wear a head covering.

of course, I said no, and let it go. Now, though, I was reading about dozens of lawsuits all around the world against the church, by adults who said they were abused by members as children. The headquarters knew about it, told the victims to not contact the police, and unless there was another witness to corroborate the claim of abuse, they would have to "leave it in Jehovah's hands." Nobody dared go to the police for fear of instant disfellowship, and the abusers continued on as members of the church, molesting more children without consequence until many years later. We never heard about these cases as witnesses. In recent years, Watchtower has been consistently losing court battles and being forced to pay out millions of dollars in restitution to victims. As such, there has been more public scrutiny by the mainstream media, but members of the religion are ordered not to watch those news reports—after all, they are just lies made up by apostates.

The final piece of the puzzle was reading *Combatting Cult Mind Control* by Steven Hassan. Hassan was brainwashed into the Moonies as a young man growing up in the seventies. Later deprogrammed, he became a psychologist and leading expert in cults, helping victims and their families. In the book, Hassan teaches that cults employ the BITE model, which stands for *behaviour*, *information*, *thoughts*, and *emotions*; cults control all these aspects of a member's life.

- **Behaviour.** As a Jehovah's Witness, dependency and blind obedience to the "faithful slave," or Governing Body, is demanded. You're told who you can spend time with, how you should act, what style of clothing you're allowed to wear, what TV shows, movies, and music you're allowed to consume, and what holidays you're allowed to observe. Your time is not yours to do with as you please—you must attend three separate two-hour meetings each week and a bare minimum of ten hours of preaching per month. Almost all your free time outside of work, school, meetings, and preaching is to be spent in studying *Watchtower* publications. You're not allowed to accept a blood transfusion, even if it means sacrificing your life. Any outside interests and talents you possess, like art, music, and sports, are never to be pursued as a career; they must be sacrificed in service to "the kingdom." Cults create their own vocabulary. Common words that are widely understood to mean one thing to the general public mean a completely different thing within the group. You've already heard me use some of these redefined words: "worldly," "field service," "brother," "slave," "truth," "apostate," "pioneer," "publisher," "disfellowshipped," "disassociated"—none of these words means what you probably think it does. Chances are, if you were a fly on the wall at a midweek meeting at the Kingdom Hall, you'd have no idea what the hell people were talking about. Another example is how

Scientologists use words like "auditing," "clear," "disconnection," and "fair game," which all have their own unique meaning specific to that group.
- **Information.** Cults control the information their members receive. The Watchtower heavily discourages non-cult sources of information among their followers, referring to the internet, radio, TV, books, and other forms of media as "a part of Satan's world." It extensively uses propaganda to keep its members in a constant state of indoctrination. Famous for their *Watchtower* and *Awake!* magazines, the Governing Body is also creating online videos to broadcast messages to their flock. As previously mentioned, Jehovah's Witnesses rewrite their own history, as well as misquoting scientists to suit their purpose, and paint all negative information about the religion, especially from former members, as lies from the devil.
- **Thoughts.** Cults form a black-and-white, us versus them kind of mentality in their members. Nonmembers are to be avoided if possible. To leave the safe haven of the group means certain death. Members are not allowed to associate with worldly people (non-Witnesses) outside of work or school unless it is strictly with the purpose of converting them. Jehovah's Witnesses internalize their beliefs as unquestionable truth, not open to any scrutiny or debate. When they speak amongst themselves, they don't call it a "reli-

gion," they call it "the truth." You "came in the truth" or "fell out of the truth." You "know the truth" and "were taught the truth." Thinking certain thoughts are a sin for which you must beg God for forgiveness.

- **Emotions.** I learned how cults manipulate the emotions of their followers, keeping them in a constant state of guilt, unworthiness, and fear. They use recruitment tactics like "love bombing," where newly interested recruits are smothered in love and acceptance by members of the cult in order to make them feel like they're part of a loving family (remember why the elderly witness couple asked me to spend time with Ricky?). Shortly after committing to the religion, however, the member realizes that the love was conditional, and they'll need to work harder and harder if they wish to keep receiving approval from fellow members. If they start missing meetings, they just might not get invited to the next Sunday barbecue. Leave for good or commit a sin, like smoking, murder, adultery, or celebrating Christmas (yes, Watchtower actually considers all of those to be equally immoral and deserving of the same punishment within the religion), and you'll be shunned by everyone in the faith, including your own family.

As I put it all together, a light came on for me—I was raised in a cult. Holy shit. This community and belief system I'd been born into and raised to believe was the only true religion, was actually a cult. I'd been raised in a doomsday cult.

TELLING MY TRUTH

I tried to wait for the right time to talk to Paula about my realization, but I found it hard not to share it. I spilled it all. Her first reaction was to go in the opposite direction; for a while she tried harder than ever to be a good Jehovah's Witness. But on some level, she understood what I was saying. As she listened to me, she was starting to awaken as well.

So far, so good. Next up, my mother. I was naïve enough to think that she, too, would welcome my revelation. It seemed so logical. All the facts were there; I just needed to lay out the case for my mother, and surely she'd see it as well.

I wrote her a mammoth email describing all the things I had discovered, explaining all the reasons Jehovah's Witnesses can't be the one true religion as they claim. The scandals, the false predictions, the commonalities with other cults. I fully expected her to call me after she read it, saying, "Oh my God, we need to talk. I can't believe you found this out."

I should have known better. Instead of embracing the

knowledge I'd shared, she immediately forwarded it to the elders, then replied to me with a short email: "How dare you make me choose between you and Jehovah. Jehovah's going to win every time. I'll never speak to you again." Later I learned she implored Paula to leave me and take Micah.

SHUNNED

My sister had the same reaction. She said she'd never talk to me again. That's what members are programmed to say and do. Shunning is an automatic reaction to claims like mine. At one point, I learned secondhand that my sister had been in the hospital with a serious, life-threatening condition and was instructed by an elder not to tell me.

My mother and I did speak a few times. I thought pleading my case in person would help but it just devolved into a shouting match. There was no convincing her.

I knew I couldn't convince the elders. Now that they knew I'd become an apostate, they would call a judicial committee, where I would sit alone with three elders. The judicial committee is treated like a court hearing, except the defendant has no witnesses or recourse at all; it's more like a kangaroo court. Its only real purpose is to make the person confess. Confess your crime and you get away with a public shaming, but you get to stay in the community. Deny it and you get disfellowshipped. It's some straight up *Game of Thrones* shit.

I couldn't "confess" to anything. Some people lie their way through the judicial committee in order to stay in the community with their friends and family. I knew that I couldn't live my life looking over my shoulder, wondering if somebody saw me doing something else that might be a disfellowshipping offence, like celebrating Christmas. Instead, I wrote my own disassociation letter.[11] In this way, they didn't get to fire me. I quit.

Handing in that letter was such a relief. I'd felt for so long like I was on the fence about everything. Now, I felt like I had finally made a move and chosen a side. Despite the fallout with my family, I slept like a baby.

LIFE AFTER FAITH

Being shunned wasn't easy. It hurt when I saw people I had once considered my spiritual brothers and sisters look away when passing by in a grocery store. I missed my mother. At the same time, I got support from the most important people in my life. Kevin was there for me. Ricky had studied but never become a baptized member

---

[11] Some jargon here: disfellowshipping is when the elders kick you out, disassociation is when you formally leave. In both cases, the result is the same: an elder reads your name to the congregation as one who is no longer a Jehovah's Witness and everyone is expected to shun you until further notice.

of the religion, so he had an even better idea of what I was going through.

Still, it's hard to really know what it's like unless you've been through the same thing. I thought about Joel Kelly. Joel and I had been in the same congregation while I was a ministerial servant, but he and his brother had left without ever explaining why. I'd seen him at some local business events since then—Joel is a digital marketer—so I decided to ask him out to coffee and see if he would talk about it.

I got right to the point, telling him I had left the religion. He visibly relaxed; I think he had been worried I was going to try to bring him back in. Not only was Joel empathetic about my leaving, he gave me resources—a Jehovah's Witness recovery forum, a sub-Reddit of ex-Jehovah's Witnesses, and perhaps best of all, his copy of *The Greatest Show on Earth*, by Richard Dawkins. It was a revelation after being sheltered from science in a religion that didn't recognize evolution.

I started questioning everything. Not just the Bible but every lesson the cult had taught me. For instance, I grew up believing that we were living in the last days, but as long as I stuck with Jehovah's people, I'd make it through Armageddon to the paradise on earth, and I would never die. I was twenty-nine before I realized everyone is going to die. Most kids figure that out at, like, ten or something.

I was shattered. I had no religion anymore, just a void, a kind of existential dread. If there wasn't a wise, loving father in the sky, what did it all mean? How are we even on earth; why are we here? Eventually, I stopped trying to believe in an afterlife or a purpose beyond what we do by being good people, having a laugh, building a legacy, spending time with people we love, doing good for the community, and helping other people along the way. I reached a point where that seemed like a good reason to be alive.[12]

REBUILDING MY LIFE

It was about five months from the day my father died to the day I left the cult. Unable to reconcile our differences, Paula and I separated again a few months later and I immersed myself in the ex-Jehovah's Witness community. For years, it seemed like something was always going wrong. If business was great, Paula and I would have a crisis. If things seemed stable at home, the business would be on the brink of closing down.

During all of this, Headspace was actually doing fine—it was growing, we had decent cash flow and lots of cli-

---

[12] While I consider myself an atheist, one who doesn't believe in the supernatural, I have no disrespect for those who do. My wife, Christina, is a believer. If your belief gives you hope and makes you a better person, I'm glad for you. Personally, I'm happier without it.

ents coming in the door to hire us. It was time for me to refocus.

Earlier, I wrote about the importance of building a business to be self-sustaining, a machine that works without you. Then, if you're going through a personal trauma like I was, you can take a leave of absence. During that period of time, I didn't feel I had that option.

While I immersed myself in the business every day, I still carved out time for therapy, dealt with my grief, and reevaluated my marriage. I also started exploring the world, doing things I wanted to do, things that were forbidden by the Jehovah's Witnesses, like growing a beard. (Every male ex-Jehovah's Witness does this. I call it my Freedom Beard.)

I also got a tattoo—just one, but it covers one side of my whole forearm. It's a woodcut illustration of a ship in a storm. It's a reminder that all problems are temporary. You can weather the storm.

CHAPTER SIX

KNOW WHEN TO FOLD 'EM

I'd love to report that everything turned around after I left the confines of the Jehovah's Witnesses. Of course, that's not what happened. To start 2013, Paula and I got back together one more time for the children, especially now that she had left the religion, too, but that didn't work out; we're just fundamentally too different from each other. We broke up for the third and final time in early 2014 after another unhappy year together.

My other relationships suffered, too. I was experiencing post-cult trauma syndrome. Yes, that's a real thing. After exiting a cult, an individual may experience a period of intense and often conflicting emotions. The victim may feel relief to be out of the group, but may also feel grief over the loss of positive elements in the cult, such as friendships, a sense of belonging, or the feeling of personal worth generated by the group's stated ideals or mission.

For me, I was angry that my mother and sister were shunning me. I had no other family nearby. I was angry that I had been deceived by the Watchtower for so long. Most of my childhood outside of school was spent attending meetings, studying for meetings, and knocking on strangers' doors. I had lost out on some of the most enjoyable aspects of being a kid that most people get to experience: friendships with "worldly" schoolmates; Christmas, Halloween, and birthday celebrations; extracurricular activities and sports; and dating in my teen years. I'll never be a kid again and get to experience those things. Now here I was, thirty years old, in a miserable marriage, in debt and chained financially to a failing business. While I had Kevin to lean on, he was dealing with his own personal problems and both of us were depressed. I felt completely, utterly alone.

I took my frustrations out on people in my personal life and in the business. I was quick-tempered and argumentative with my clients and staff. I enjoyed debating with people about religion and politics in person and on YouTube and Facebook (recovering troll here). One time, I wrote a scathing email to a lead who I had thought was signing my proposal for a new website project but backed out unexpectedly.

I had a lot to learn about managing relationships. The only people who were truly honest with me about it were Paula and Ricky. They both told me in so many words, "Kyle, you're an asshole. But not deep down; we know you can change."

When I finally read Dale Carnegie's classic book, *How to Win Friends and Influence People*, I couldn't believe what I was reading; Use your opponent's momentum against them? Instead of fighting, agree with them? It seemed like a Jedi mind trick. Eventually I did learn; it's much easier to convince somebody they are wrong if you present it in a nonargumentative way, so they come to the right conclusion themselves instead of you trying to force them to it.

I use these principles today when talking to my employees in a one-on-one. I avoid criticizing them specifically because I know people shut down when they hear what sounds like condemnation. Instead, I praise them sincerely and tell them what I appreciate about their work. Then I talk about a shared problem we both have so it's not me against them, it's us against the world. I suggest some possible ways the person may be able to better contribute to solving the problem. It almost always results in the employee taking it to heart and improving their performance in that area.

Developing these skills didn't happen right away but, gradually, I was able to move on from my post-cult trauma and improve my communication with other people.

HOW NOT TO SELL A BUSINESS

At that time, Headspace was still experiencing irregular cash flow. Some months were fine and other times Kevin would still need to drive somewhere to pick up a cheque so we could make payroll.

At the same time, Proposify was trying to raise money. We'd attracted the attention of Innovacorp, an early stage venture capital firm in Halifax. We had this fantasy in our heads that if we could just get an investor to put a million dollars in an account, we could continue to run the agency and develop our product for Proposify. Of course, it's never that easy. After some discussion, we got turned down for the investment by Innovacorp. They felt we were too early with our product and were nervous putting money into a service business like ours. They were right to reject us at that time—the easiest thing to do when your startup isn't gaining traction is to go back to what you know makes you money: client work. Investors know that.

We knew we had to transition out of Headspace. Probably the easiest thing to do would have been to file for bankruptcy, lay everyone off, and screw over our remaining clients, banker, and landlord, but that would have been a dishonourable way to go out. We wanted to make the most graceful exit possible, and to do right by our employees, clients, and banker. So Kevin started talking candidly to people about buying our agency.

NOT SO FAST

In the fall of 2013, we got a bite on Headspace. Out of nowhere, a former client from when I worked at Impact called me. His name is Peter, the founder and CEO of a company called Stright-MacKay, a marine parts distributor in Nova Scotia. If you have a boat and need to buy a bilge pump, chances are you'll buy it from the Stright-MacKay catalogue. He told me he had been watching Headspace for years and wanted to buy a marketing agency to work on his website and print materials. It looked like a good deal for both of us. We wanted out, and they had the resources to turn Headspace around and come out with a valuable company.

Everything went smoothly at first. Peter said he was bringing in a partner named Jim, who ran an e-learning business, to go in on the deal with him. Jim knew a lot more about digital marketing than Peter did. Both would bring the cash but Jim would run the business. So far, so good.

We agreed on basic terms up front; it would be an asset purchase, not a share purchase. What that means is, instead of buying the shares in our corporation, they would buy our corporation's assets and transfer them to a new corporation. Headspace owed the bank $150,000, so an asset purchase would release them from any liabilities associated with our existing corporation. The assets included our client projects, accounts receivable, proprietary software, employees, brand name, website, and whatever equipment we owned, like desks and computers. In return, they would pay us $300,000 in cash. We would use that to pay off the bank and each net $75,000 personally. Since we had carved Proposify out into its own corporation and they didn't want it, we got to keep it. This was an amazing deal for us.

We got the lawyers on it. As anyone who has ever brought lawyers into a deal knows, they can drag things out. Waiting for their lawyer to draft something would sometimes take weeks. Then we'd need to wait for our lawyer to review it and book a call with us. We'd hop on a call with him and he would hem and haw about a particular term in their contract that might not give us absolute protection in an extreme circumstance down the road. We kept telling him, "We need this deal to happen! We don't care!

We'll accept the consequences!" We were indeed desperate. We were trying to keep Proposify going even though we had barely any customers, and we were trying to pay everyone on Headspace's staff—we knew if we laid everybody off, we wouldn't have anything to sell.

The problem was, the bank had a hold on our assets because of money we owed them. We signed away control when we borrowed money from them. So we took the deal to our special loans banker at RBC and tried to appeal to his common sense: if the deal didn't happen, the bank would never get its money back. If, on the other hand, the bank released the assets and formed a new agreement with us, we could close the deal and pay RBC back. It sounded reasonable to us, but not to Dave. Dave was in special loans, and like "Big Tony," who the mafia sends in to break legs, he wasn't here to make friends. He told us outright, "I don't care about people like you, I care about RBC's shareholders." Dave didn't make deals with scum like us, who borrowed money to build a business and then struggled. He seemed to have a personal vendetta against us and wanted us to fail.

We didn't know what to do. We were at a stalemate with the purchasers, who were increasingly becoming less interested in this floundering business. As time dragged on, Peter was squeezing us, hoping to push us into a desperate position so we'd give away the business for nothing.

As it turned out, we *would* eventually give the business away. In the end, we didn't make a cent from the sale.

In late 2013, Kevin told me Proposify had been accepted into the Canadian Technology Accelerator. I didn't really know what that was, but he said it was a good opportunity he had applied for a while back. In March 2014, Kevin and I drove to Boston from Nova Scotia, a ten-hour drive. On the way there, we received a call from Jim. Peter was backing out. We nearly passed out. After we had a moment to digest the news, Jim offered a silver lining. He was still interested; he really wanted Extrify, our SaaS product, he just didn't have the funds to buy it. So we worked out a deal where Jim would take over running Headspace, pay our employees and operating expenses, and deposit payments from clients into his account. Over time, he would pay back our debts to everyone but RBC. It wasn't ideal but it was better than nothing. So far, it was a gentleman's agreement; nobody had signed anything yet. I know, I know. Always have a contract. That's good advice.

The $3,000 a month fee Jim paid us each as contractors to continue working on Headspace wasn't quite enough to pay our personal bills, so I took on outside freelance work to supplement the rest. With no contract, and thus no agreed-upon end date, this nightmare of a deal was still going on well into March 2014, without an end in sight. We counted it as progress, though; at least we had one foot outside the agency and could begin to believe it was possible to exit the business.

HOW TO SELL A BUSINESS

The number one lesson we learned selling Headspace was that you need to know what your agency is worth. To sell the business properly, we should have gotten a handle on our value long before the sale, but the way we were running things made that nearly impossible. Assessing your value should be straightforward—if your annual revenue is a million dollars, you should be able to get one or two million in a sale, depending on how profitable you are, what your margins look like, how quickly you're growing, and whether you're in debt. Our finances were in chaos; we didn't have any of that information squared away. (We hired accountants who did such terrible jobs with our books it was difficult to even deliver an up-to-date balance sheet to potential acquirers.)

The number two lesson we learned was that you need to build a turnkey business. Our main problem was that Kevin and I brought in most of the business ourselves and did much of the work. Without us in the business, there wasn't much left. To make a successful sale, you need to make sure your business is valuable without you. A turnkey business is one you can hand over to someone else because you've created a system anyone can come in and run.

You should also ask for help. Get experienced accountants and lawyers on board during the sale. They can see the big picture that you probably can't. Our lawyer at Proposify, Rob Cowen at McInnes Cooper, for example, has been amazing when doing deals—he's responsive, sees the big picture, and keeps the deal moving forward until we can seal it.

Get your network on board, too. Leveraging your connections can be more effective, and less expensive, than depending on a broker. Don't forget your competitors are part of your network, too. Sometimes competitors will want to buy up your agency just so they can take your clients and team and add them to theirs.

With connections, due diligence, and some luck, you'll make the sale, better than we did. Then what? While you're embroiled in the sales process, you can't neglect planning for your next move.

I didn't do that, partly because I was somewhat uncomfortable about getting out of the business completely. I had built an identity around running an agency and being a UX expert. What would people think of me now? I had to let go of that concern in order to move forward.

SUMMER OF HELL

I remember the summer of 2013, the worst summer of my life. In addition to all the other stress happening around me with the Peter and Jim deal, something else happened. One day, I looked at my personal finances and saw a transaction from my bank account for several thousand dollars. Confused, I asked Paula, who at first said she didn't know about it, but when I pressed her, she admitted she had taken cash out to pay for a trip for herself and her teenage daughter. Here I was busting my ass to bring in enough money so she didn't have to work, we were struggling to pay our rent, and yet she'd snuck money out for a frivolous vacation!

In my anger, I kicked the nearest inanimate object I could find: my dresser. As soon as I did I heard a snap, and I couldn't walk. Paula took me to the hospital, and after X-rays I learned that I had broken the base of my big toe and would need to be in a cast. The cast was applied tightly and I was in such discomfort for days that I went back to the hospital. After an ultrasound, it turned out that the cast was so tight it had caused a blood clot in my leg, and then later my lung. There was a risk I would have a pulmonary embolism, where a clot goes to your lung, causing you to die. They took the cast off, which was a relief, but I was still on crutches for months. Now I would need to be put on Warfarin, blood-thinning medication, and for a week, I needed daily Fragmin injections, painful needles in the belly. I was terrified of dying from the blood clot. Lesson learned: choose soft objects to kick.

During that summer, I took six-year-old Micah to the lake to swim. I sat on the dock and thought about my life. Maybe Headspace was over. Maybe my entrepreneurial career was, too? Proposify was on the horizon. We had a basic product and a handful of customers, plus Jonathan was continually working on it. I was skeptical after everything we had been through but Kevin tried to talk me into it. He was sure it was going to be a huge success. I sat there considering parting ways with Kevin to try to run the agency myself. He and Jonathan could continue with Proposify if they wanted. In the end, I decided to continue on with Kevin and Proposify.

FACING THE MUSIC

It didn't come easily. For a long time, my finances were a complete mess—I could barely pay my rent. One day, both my personal bank account and my business account happened to be overdrawn, and I had no cash on me. So when crossing the bridge between Dartmouth and Halifax, I literally didn't have enough money to pay the bridge toll. I waited for a car to go through, and tailgated behind it so I could squeeze through. As I drove over the bridge, I thought to myself, "What happened to get you to this place, where you can't afford a bridge token?"

I was reduced to building WordPress sites on the side to supplement my small Headspace fee. I was between payments and I needed to pay rent, which was about $1,300. There wasn't enough to cover it, and I had already been late on payments before. I swallowed my pride and asked my aunt to loan me $1,000 for two days to pay my landlord. She turned me down. It further sank in how alone I truly was.

Most business owners I knew did well financially. Even in my Jehovah's Witness congregation there were some men who owned businesses, and they were usually well off. I thought entrepreneurship meant never being broke. It's supposed to be sexy. In reality, it requires patience and the ability to put your head down and work and learn for a long period of time before you even begin to see any wealth.

Remember that picture of Jeff Bezos taken in the late 1990s? It showed him in a miserable office with bad fluorescent lighting, grey carpet, and a poorly designed Amazon logo on the wall, printed on a Bubble Jet printer. He was wearing a button-down collared shirt, working on a clunky-looking yellow PC. Nothing about the picture was sexy. But he was working.

That's the true entrepreneur people should know about. True entrepreneurs are dedicated to building something meaningful; they don't care if they look glamorous in the meantime. Most successful entrepreneurs are poor until they're not. Fortunately, I was always drawn to being able to control my own destiny more than glamour. For me, becoming an entrepreneur was all about being able to do it on my own.

In a way, I was lucky to have not been successful right away. If wealth had come easily, I may have taken it for granted. I learned by necessity that the best way to get rich is to focus on creating value for people—solving somebody's problem in the best, most helpful way possible. That isn't to say that entrepreneurial success has nothing to do with money. It does. The mark of a good entrepreneur is being able to extract money from customers and generate revenue, just like being a good football player means scoring touchdowns. You need to market and sell. If you're working on a business for years and years and it isn't making money, you need to know when to quit!

At the same time, if you chase money, it eludes you. But if you focus on solving problems for people, money will somehow make its way to you as a result. You just need the grit and determination to keep going even when it gets beyond hard.

PART III
REBIRTH

CHAPTER SEVEN

THE TIDES CHANGE

It was just after Christmas in late December 2013. Around this time of year in the northern hemisphere, the weather cools off and it gets dark around four in the afternoon.

My foot was still broken. My finances were in the toilet. Headspace was struggling to keep its head above water. I was working twelve-hour days on both the agency and my own freelancing to keep my bills paid. The nightmare deal with Jim and Peter showed no signs of closing. I was depressed. I even submitted my résumé to an agency in North Carolina for a design position—Paula and I were literally discussing moving to the US. It didn't matter; I got rejected for the job because they didn't sponsor immigrants.

On a lark, I signed up for a local pitch competition, if

anything to get out of the house. Volta, the local startup workspace, held monthly pitch competitions, where five or so startups pitch for five minutes each. Two local judges pick a winner. In January 2014, I stood up in front of a small crowd and pitched Proposify, showing that we were building proposal software to help agencies close more deals, we had about ten customers, we knew a little bit more about what we were selling, and we were getting some positive feedback.

I won the competition, but I didn't realize that this was a turning point for me and the business, because an associate from Innovacorp named Ken Lee, the same VC group that rejected us a year prior, was in the audience, and was impressed by the progress we'd made. After the event, Kevin and I spent time talking to Ken and demoing our product to him. He was going to bring it to his colleagues and get us a meeting with Greg Phipps, someone higher up in the firm. As I mentioned in the last chapter, Kevin got us accepted into a three-month accelerator in Boston—the Canadian Technology Accelerator—and Ken was especially impressed that we got into it. This was one of those life-changing moments, the one where you wonder to yourself, "If I had decided not to show up that day, would my life be the same today?"

SIGNS OF SPRING

Kevin and I left for Boston. Since we both had families and children, we agreed that I would stay for March, he for April, and then I'd go back in May to finish it. At that point in time, I hadn't travelled a lot, so I pictured Boston as it was portrayed in movies like *The Departed*. I half expected Jack Nicholson's character, Frank Costello, to empty a round into me if I stepped foot in Beantown.

My experience ended up being much more mundane. Kevin and I made the ten-hour drive and stayed with some of his relatives for a few days before finding a place for me called Krashpad, where other startup founders and students stay for short periods of time.

The particular location I was staying at was in Charlestown, the same town in Ben Affleck's *The Town*. Oh my God, I am totally going to get murdered by a bank-robbing Jeremy Renner here! Kevin dropped me off with my suitcase under a bridge in a rundown area of town, and made his way back to Nova Scotia, forlornly looking back at me in his rearview mirror. He said he felt like he was dropping his son off to college.

At thirty, I was one of the oldest people in Krashpad. Most were in their twenties and studying programming at MIT or Harvard. The Canadian Technology Accelerator (CTA) program itself was underwhelming. I would commute on the T from Charlestown to Cambridge and work out of the Cambridge Innovation Centre. The CTA "program" was pretty much nonexistent; I was assigned a desk and got an email newsletter every week telling me what business events were going on in town. I worked long days and nights by myself on Headspace, Proposify, and my freelance work to pay the bills back home. I would get on FaceTime with the kids every night. I missed my boys terribly. While the program itself was a dud, I met a lot of great people from all over the US, Canada, and Europe, some of whom I'm still in contact with.

One positive note: I had the opportunity to work with a pitch coach named Linda Plano on better ways to pitch Proposify to investors. The coaching must have worked; when I flew back to Nova Scotia in April to make a pitch to Innovacorp's board of directors, we got a green light. A $250,000 investment! That, plus a $20,000 investment from another contact of mine, named Patrick Hankinson, who had just sold his company Compilr to linda.com, and matching interest-free loan from the Atlantic Canada Opportunities Agency, and we had about half a million dollars in investments. Days before, I had been struggling to pay rent, and now it looked like we had a fighting chance! It took another couple of months before the deal finalized, but by May when I returned to Boston, the money hit our account.

STARS ALIGN

The turnaround felt like a long time coming, but it was amazing how the stars aligned when the change came. Not only did we have the investment deal closed, that same week we managed to pin Jim down on the purchase and sale agreement for Headspace. He had been putting us off for months; there was always a reason why he couldn't sign it that particular day. So one day, Kevin and I ambushed him while we were getting drinks on the patio of the sushi restaurant next to Headspace to celebrate the deal. We saw Jim walking by the office and called out to him, and invited him to sit down to grab a drink with us. When he did, we pulled out the printed purchase and sale agreement and practically ordered him to sign it. To our amazement, he did. And just like that, Headspace was sold.

The Proposify investment closed. The Headspace purchase and sale closed. Next, Paula sat me down and suggested we separate amicably—this time it was permanent. It sounds awful but it was a huge relief to me. Paula was the only woman I had ever been with, but I had been miserable with her for the last six years of our marriage. I longed to be single and date other people. I would support her and we would share custody of the kids and try to make it as painless as possible for them, but we both knew this was better for everyone.

I went back to Boston in May, but there wasn't much to worry about. For the first time, I was single in a city. I felt like I was twenty years old. I met up with my Krashpad friends at a dive bar on the first night I landed, and we celebrated the deal closing. I met a woman there named Becky and we exchanged phone numbers. She was the first woman I had been with since Paula and we had a fun, short-lived romance. That month I worked solely on Proposify each day in Cambridge and saw Becky in the evenings. The spring weather was warm in Boston. Everything was new again, and I let go of all the baggage I'd held for so long. It felt like a whole new chapter of life had begun.

MORE LESSONS LEARNED

The first lesson to take away from this period is that you have to get out there and talk about your company. If I hadn't done my first pitch competition, who knows what would have happened? Maybe we would have found the funding another way but it was clearly a catalyst. If you're an early startup trying to get funding, get out and do as many events as you can. I know, it can seem like a waste of time. If you're an introverted developer or designer, you probably don't *want* to get out and mingle. I get it, but I learned it's worth the trouble. Do events and talk to people and you will find customers, potential investors, partners, and maybe even a cofounder.

You also have to get comfortable with risk. When you read our story, you realize this whole period was highly risky for us, financially and otherwise. It's smart to hedge your bets a bit, have a backup plan in place. (Kevin and I had our résumés out during this period). You also need to recognize that sometimes taking a risk is the only way to reap the rewards.

Finally, you have to come to terms with the possibility of having nothing. I learned that having nothing is a superpower. When you stop feeling attached to the idea of looking successful, it makes you very powerful. You gain a lot of leverage. If you have nothing to lose, you can just keep working on the idea, even when most people would have given up. You also make better decisions, because you're not making them based on the fear of losing what you have. You already have nothing, so go for it.

It's like that scene in the American version of *The Office* when Michael Scott is negotiating the sale of his eponymous paper company to Dunder Mifflin:

> Our company is worth nothing. That's the difference between you and I. Business isn't about money to me, David. If tomorrow my company goes under I will just start another paper company. And then another and another and another. I have no shortage of company names.

Even with money in the bank, Headspace sold, and Proposify on its way, we still weren't far from having nothing to lose. Kevin and I had gone into debt personally and were forced to forfeit on our personally guaranteed business loan from the bank. To protect ourselves from legal action, we each filed for a consumer proposal. A consumer proposal is one step before bankruptcy; a trustee negotiates with your creditors to consolidate your debt into a manageable monthly payment. Once the consumer proposal is finalized, creditors legally cannot come after you (as long as you make your payments). I had my debt negotiated down to only $18,000 and had to make monthly payments of $300 for five years until it was paid off. As humiliating as it was to go through that process, with no more collection agencies calling my cell phone to threaten me, I was finally able to breathe again.

We knew that we needed to pay ourselves a modest salary in order to focus on Proposify without worrying about how to take care of our families. We had very few expenses, but even so, the funds would only last ten months or so. The ten or twenty regular customers paying us maybe twenty dollars a month weren't going to make up the gap. I could get free-trial signups to our website through SEO, content, and word of mouth, but our product wasn't far enough along to be able to retain customers long term. We needed to be able to retain customers and grow our revenue soon if we were going to survive.

CHAPTER EIGHT

BUILDING PRODUCT

In July 2014, Kevin and I went to Startupfest in Montreal, where we would hear Dan Martell speak. Martell, angel investor and entrepreneur,[13] said everyone wants their growth to follow the "hockey stick" trajectory, but in order to get there you have to go through the flat period first. We knew we were in the flat period, so we decided to do everything we could to hit the corner and head up.

What we needed to round that corner was to achieve product/market fit, making sure we had the right product for the right market. Marc Lowell Andreessen, cofounder of Netscape and venture capital firm Andreessen Horow-

---

[13] As fate would have it, I hired Dan to be my business coach in 2017.

itz, wrote that there are two stages of a startup—before PM fit and after PM fit:

> When you are BPMF, focus obsessively on getting to product/market fit. Do whatever is required to get to product/market fit. Including changing out people, rewriting your product, moving into a different market, telling customers no when you don't want to, telling customers yes when you don't want to, raising that fourth round of highly dilutive venture capital—whatever is required. When you get right down to it, you can ignore almost everything else. I'm not suggesting that you do ignore everything else—just that judging from what I've seen in successful startups, you can.

We had taken that advice and done whatever it takes. We rewrote our product, raised investment, and sold our agency. But we knew that to reach PM fit we needed to do things that don't scale. That's a term coined by venture capitalist and founder of Y Combinator Paul Graham, who wrote in his now legendary blog post "Do Things That Don't Scale."

> One of the most common types of advice we give at Y Combinator is to do things that don't scale. A lot of would-be founders believe that startups either take off or don't. You build something, make it available, and if you've made a better mousetrap, people beat a path to your door as promised. Or they don't, in which case the market must

not exist. Actually startups take off because the founders make them take off. There may be a handful that just grew by themselves, but usually it takes some sort of push to get them going. A good metaphor would be the cranks that car engines had before they got electric starters. Once the engine was going, it would keep going, but there was a separate and laborious process to get it going.

That distinction is important, because you might have to do things at first that won't ultimately scale. You should still do them. Think of Airbnb hiring professional photographers to shoot photos of apartments and condos in New York City. They knew that high-quality photography would help attract people to book spaces; if people posted crappy shots they took themselves, nobody would sign up. Hiring a photographer was expensive but worth the investment. You can figure out how to scale after you've hit product/market fit, but beforehand, almost anything is fair game.

We knew we hadn't hit product/market fit in the first year, because we were still losing a customer every time we gained a customer. Taking Graham's advice to heart, we decided we had to do things that used up a lot of resources without immediately bringing in money, like spending our time talking to customers every chance we got.

We asked a lot of questions. Where did they get hung up

in the product? What would they like to see that would help solve their problem? The product didn't work for some people. It didn't solve their problems, or it was too hard to use, or they couldn't figure it out. We listened; we spent a lot of time watching customers use the product by screenshare. Not very sexy but very informative. I decided to embrace the negative feedback and treat it like a gift. After all, if they didn't tell me this stuff, how would I ever find out? I came to appreciate the people who cared enough to say, "I'm pissed. This is a piece of shit. I hate it. I left you a video—watch it not working." I watched, and I thanked them profusely.

Most people became customers for life after that. They knew we were there for them. Why else would we jump on the phone late at night to help them on a real proposal for a real client? They were thrilled that the company's founder would talk to them at midnight to help them meet a deadline.

Even if they were only paying twenty dollars a month, I gave them the white-glove service. That helped us build loyal fans while we were working out the kinks. Many of them stuck with us, but even those who didn't promoted our product to others. We learned to obsess over our clients and treat them like gold.

In late 2014, Proposify began reaching product/market

fit. In October, we had a spike in revenue and thought it was an anomaly, but by November we had doubled our MRR again, then in December doubled again. The flat part sure had been there for seventeen months, but we finally reached the hockey stick.

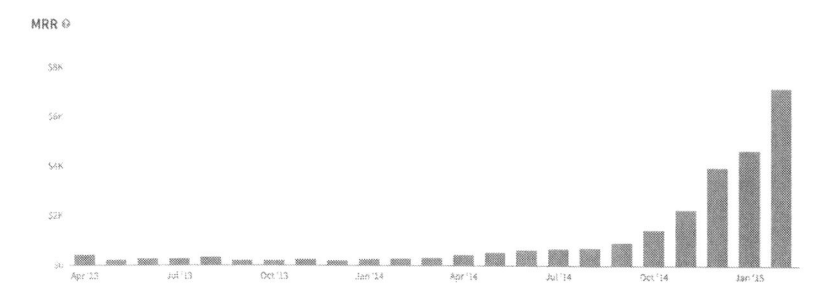

Sean Ellis, the entrepreneur, angel investor, and startup advisor who coined the term "growth hacker," created the "product/market fit survey." It's a simple survey that asks your users one question: How would you feel if you could no longer use [product]? The possible answers are:

- Very disappointed
- Somewhat disappointed
- Not disappointed (it really isn't that useful)
- NA—I no longer use this product

According to Ellis, if at least 40 percent of your respondents say they would be very disappointed if they could no longer use your product, then you've achieved an objective level of PM fit and can begin scaling. I ran the survey, with some trepidation. I was afraid of what the response would be, but we needed to know where we were at.

I shouldn't have worried. Around 60 percent said they'd be "very disappointed" if Proposify went away. The survey actually freaked some customers out because they thought we were shutting down. They refused the idea, saying things like, "If you get rid of this thing, I'm gonna fly out to Nova Scotia, wherever the hell that is, and beat you all up." That was nice to hear. On Twitter, we were getting messages like "Love Proposify! It just saved me a ton of time on a proposal" or "I just won a new proposal using Proposify."

We did it. We hit product/market fit. In January 2015, we were at about $5,000 in MRR. A year later we were at $70,000 and continuing to grow quickly, with a small team and without needing to raise more investment dollars.

DISCOVERING WHAT THE CUSTOMER WANTS

Remember when Netflix was known for sending red envelopes with DVDs to your mailbox? No? Most people don't; they only think of Netflix as online video streaming.

When Netflix started, there was no market for video

streaming. Nobody had a fast enough broadband connection. You would have thought Netflix was crazy for thinking about streaming at the time. But you'd be wrong. They were smart to think not only about what customers wanted then, but what they'd want in the future.

At Proposify, we were similarly challenged to be forward-thinking. At Headspace, we worked with government clients who used paper documents and handwritten signatures. Yet some of our users were starting to use online signatures. We started to hear from people who wanted that option. Then we noticed competitors offered it. We weren't far behind.

You never know what your customers will want until they tell you their problem. We realized that a huge hurdle for a lot of our users was in getting their existing proposals into our software. At first I tried doing things that don't scale and manually importing it for them. But I realized that to really start growing our revenue we needed a more scalable way. Working with Jonathan, I came up with a new templating system that was easier to use and I designed about ten high quality proposal templates that users could click to import into their account. *Ease of Use

You have to make it easy on your customers. If you don't, they're history. Think of Mint, the online service that gathers your banking information and categorizes it so you know where your money is going. They're the most popular such service but they weren't the first. A competitor called Wasabi came up with the idea, but they made a crucial miscalculation: they expected customers to manually categorize their expenses to be more accurate. Mint, on the other hand, categorized the data automatically, even though it was less accurate. You probably can guess how this turned out: Wasabi shut down and Mint sold to Intuit for $170 million in just two years.

Needless to say, we created templates for our clients at Proposify.

> We kept doing discovery, and we do it to this day. When customers sign up for a trial, we send them an email saying, "Hey, thanks for signing up for your free trial of Proposify. Why did you sign up? Knowing why people sign up helps us make sure that we're delivering what they need."

[margin note: ask people why they sign up. for free trial.]

We get a healthy number of responses from these emails. Some respond because they're excited about signing up. They're in a good frame of mind to give feedback. They'll tell us things like "Oh, I was really struggling with streamlining my proposal process," which was valuable information. Now we knew how the customer defined their problem, and it wasn't what we were saying on our marketing site. We were saying, "Create beautiful proposals." Streamlining is a little different. When we started using our customers' language on our marketing site, we got even higher conversion. Talk like your customers do.

PICK ONE METRIC THAT MATTERS

Many startup founders try to optimize every part of their funnel at the same time, generating people at the top of the funnel, buying ads, and doing SEO or whatever it takes to get people visiting their website. The problem with this approach is that it's no use filling the funnel if the product is not right. That rarely works. Instead, think about one metric that you can work on right now that will actually move the needle on the business.

I got this idea from a book I recommend to all entrepreneurs: *Lean Analytics*, co-authored by Ben Yoskovitz, who later became one of our board members. According to Ben, there are five stages of every startup: empathy, stickiness, virality, revenue, and growth. You need to focus on the one metric that matters *right now* to get you from one stage to the next. For example, don't work on changing pricing plans (revenue), or focusing on a ton of traffic (acquisition), when you don't even have a product that will keep people around (stickiness). Keeping to the discipline of paying attention to the metric that mattered helped us a lot with Proposify. Even though I was doing a lot of marketing work on the side to drive site visits, we were mostly focused on building a product that people cared about and wanted to use.

SKIP THE PIVOT

When we were struggling in 2014, there was always the temptation to change direction, to pivot. The startup world talks a lot about pivots, such as how Twitter started as a podcasting app, Odeo, then pivoted to providing a way to send a short SMS messages (and now allows the president of the United States to tweet from his golden toilet at three in the morning). Or how Tiny Speck pivoted from failing online game Glitch into the fastest growing startup of all time, the messaging app Slack. When people hear these successful pivot stories, they think pivoting is a must. If things aren't working out right away, you either apply your product to a new market or keep the same market and build a different product to solve a different problem.

One of the best decisions we made was to *not* pivot. It took more discipline to stay focused and stick to what we knew. We knew we were solving the right problem. We knew people were searching for it. We knew they were signing up to trials. We just couldn't convert them, or if we did, we couldn't retain them. We didn't need to go in a new direction; we needed to take a new approach to the landscape we were already in.

ADDING FEATURES

Once we started doubling our revenue after some months, we had a new problem: hundreds of feature requests. Which ones do we add to the product?

It was tempting, but product development needs to be managed carefully. As you get more customers, you get more feedback. When thousands of customers request new features every day, you have to figure out what's smart to build and what's not. The goal of product management is not to constantly build new things, but to build the right thing at the right time.

We had to realize that just because a customer asks for something, we didn't have to provide it. Often, we can make them happy without it. Listen closely, and you'll find that most customers aren't asking for a new feature, necessarily. What they really want is for you to solve their problem. For example, at Proposify, our users kept asking for a separate table of contents feature. We couldn't figure out why. Our software was built to send the proposal out as a link, by email. The recipient then opens it in a web browser, and voilà, a table of contents automatically appears. That seemed fine to us.

It turned out our customers were worried the proposal wouldn't show up correctly when their client opened it. They didn't trust the web preview. So they downloaded

PDFs of their proposals and manually emailed them to clients, which meant they would lose out on a lot of the features that make Proposify useful, like e-signatures, video, interactive pricing options, and knowing which sections their clients spent the most time on. So we asked, what if we gave them a better way of testing it out themselves before sending? They said that was perfect. Problem solved. Understanding what customers *really need*, not what they *ask for*, meant we got out of building an unnecessary feature and were able to add more value to the product in the ways that mattered most.

We weren't always so wise. We built some features that seemed obvious to us, like the find-and-replace feature we built into the earliest version of Proposify, but people didn't really use it. If they did, they didn't like it. The resources we spent building the feature could have been better used elsewhere. We took it out and replaced it with Variables, which allows you to enter short codes into your text, like {client_name}, which automatically pulls in the appropriate client name for that proposal.

Product management is more of an art than a science. Having years of experience as a user-experience designer and marketer, and understanding our initial target audience of small agency owners was certainly helpful in getting to product/market fit. A lot of product management is in having a vision for your product, knowing whom you're building it for, and making decisions based on what customers are begging for *and* what aligns with your vision. I've found over the years, though, that there are some more objective ways to decide what to build.

FEATURE AUDIT

As your product grows, you need to be careful about what features you add because they'll always take longer to build than you think, and once they're built you'll need to continue to refine what you've built, measuring usage, making it easier to use, and fixing related bugs.

Sometimes it's obvious what feature to build, like the templates and online signatures, but sometimes it's not so you have to prioritize. One method for figuring that out is to build a graph with X and Y axes, where you list your top five "to be built" features. The X axis represents the percentage of your users who will use the product, and the Y axis represents how often they will use it. The idea is that a feature *all of your users* will use *all of the time* is a no-brainer. A feature that some of your users will use all of the time, or most of your users will use most of the time is still worthy of consideration, but anything outside of that should be considered very carefully.

THE TYPICAL FEATURE AUDIT

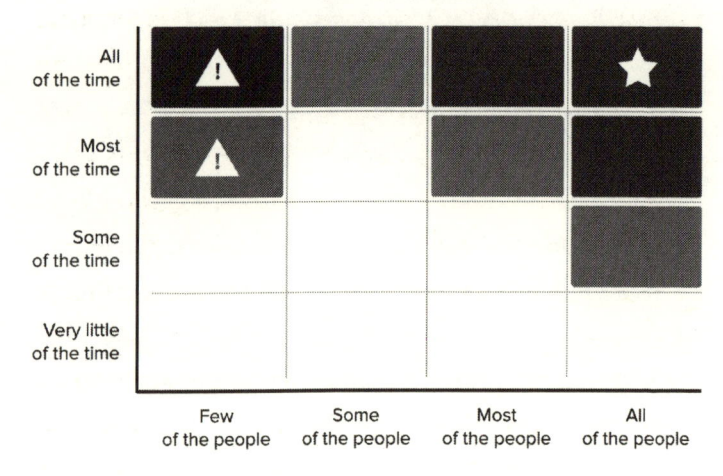

ICE SCORE

Another product development framework we like to use is Scott Ellis's ICE score. It was originally created to plan out growth experiments but I've found it a useful way to prioritize many types of projects, including feature development.

ICE stands for *impact*, *confidence*, and *ease of implementation*. With this method, you list possible features and score them on a scale of five, answering these questions:

1. **Impact.** What is the impact this feature would have? Would it really move the needle on the business? Would it really differentiate us? Would people freak out (in a good way) over this kind of thing? Will it have a huge impact?

2. **Confidence.** How confident are you that it will have that kind of impact? Is this based on qualitative data or is it just a shower thought?
3. **Ease of implementation.** How easy will this be to build? If it's something that can be built, tested, and released in one development sprint, it may be worth taking a risk to test and learn what the market thinks.

The score helps you figure out where to focus your efforts and how to move features up the chain. Features that you're *highly confident* will have a *massive impact* and are *relatively easy* to implement should come first. Of course, there are no silver bullets, but these frameworks are useful for gut checks. They let you test your assumptions and provide information that can help you decide what to build.

HANG ON TO PRODUCT/MARKET FIT

As your product evolves, you face another challenge—keeping the product/market fit you worked so hard to attain. Every successful company in the world has met product/market fit once, but not all of them can maintain it. Blockbuster once had a great PM fit in the video-rental market. Those customers didn't disappear but they evolved. No longer would they walk into a store on a Friday night, wait in line hoping to snag the newest releases, and agree to pay late fees if they forgot to return the DVDs the next day. Why go through all that when they had streaming video at home? Blockbuster didn't keep up with the changing market. Sears once had PM fit, too, and was the Amazon of its day for over a century—until the actual Amazon came along and dominated e-commerce, leaving Sears struggling for survival.

At a startup, constant development doesn't seem like a big problem, because you can make big changes very quickly. But as your customers scale, bringing with them more bug reports and greater infrastructure pressure, among other things, your feature development slows down. Paradoxically, as a company gets bigger and has more resources, it also gets slower and struggles to adapt to change.

The thing is, you can't stop building features. The product is never done. This is why companies need to raise money to hire more engineers to keep growing their team. Companies like Google, Microsoft, and Facebook have thousands of developers. They're never done building. But even they can't build everything. Virtual graveyards are littered with the bodies of failed products from tech giants. Facebook discontinued its email service, Google failed to create a social network people use, and Microsoft botched the Windows Phone. Suffice it to say, companies big and small need to be specific and focused about what they put into the world.

PAYING ATTENTION TO DESIGN

The best tech companies understand the importance of investing in design. If they didn't, they would risk creating a Swiss Army knife sort of product that's too complicated or clunky to use. Not every company realizes this, so investing in design is all too rare. I'm still amazed that a lot of SaaS startup founders have no background in design or UX but are trying to build products. I would never start a restaurant business with zero industry experience working in kitchens or dining rooms. New founders assume they can hire a freelancer for two weeks to create an initial design and then it's done. Not true. It's an ongoing process. Someone once asked me who created the Proposify interface. The answer is several people (first me, then Ricky, then Edison, then Genevieve) and no one; it's a product of gradual evolution over years.

Part of the problem may be that people don't always understand what design is. Design is all about maximizing the user experience. It's not how it looks; it's how it works.

Here's one of my favourite examples of UX from the book *Killer UX Design*, by Jodie Moule:

> I was in Hong Kong on a business trip and I ordered an iced coffee in the hotel lobby. The iced coffee came out and I

noticed there was ice in it. Groan. Lovers of iced coffee will know there is a fine balance between milk and coffee; putting ice in it waters down the coffee. However, when I investigated the ice cubes closely, I noticed they were made of coffee! A smart person had taken into account the problem of ice cubes watering down the coffee. This had been overcome by making ice cubes out of actual coffee, so that when they melted, the "user" was left with an equally strong coffee flavour. Brilliant!

That's how you design a product for optimal user experience—you get your product to the point where a user says, "They thought of everything. They get me."

At one time, you could probably get away with a product that was less then amazing. People would tolerate a clunky interface if the product worked. Not anymore. Buyers today will choose based on how it feels to use your product; even enterprise software has to respond to the trend and design with the user in mind.

The best way to test your design is to try it yourself. Occasionally, I've used Proposify to send a proposal to a real client, to see what it's like from an end-user standpoint. As I was using it, I thought, "Wow, that really was fast and easy. We built a nice thing." Conversely, I've also used it and run into issues. That made me feel empathy for customers who were experiencing bugs or usability issues.

DESIGNING ON A TEAM

If you're not a trained designer—and even if you are—you don't have to reinvent the wheel with each design. The components are already out there. You have to know *about* them but you don't have to be an expert in everything, especially if you work on a team with other experts.

Most designers are not engineers, but if you understand the basics of how software is built, what a database is and how it works and communicates with the server, and what markup is, that's enough for you to have a meaningful conversation with the engineers on your team. That might be all you need to know, just enough to understand the limits you face with a given design.

On occasion, I've been able to offer up (dare I say) clever technical solutions to Jonathan, my CTO, because I knew just enough to be dangerous. Developers often approach problems from the most technically sound standpoint, whereas I approach problems trying to find the quickest path from point A to point B. For example, when I wanted a way to be able to change templates on the fly, Jonathan looked at my design and told me it couldn't be done because a user would need to leave the editor, but to apply the style changes, the editor would need to be loaded (stay with me here). I suggested just faking it by throwing up a modal window over the top of the editor, so that it *looked* like the user left the editor but in reality they didn't. Jonathan thought for a second. "Oh, that works." The more you know about development, the more you can work with your engineering team to design elegant solutions to problems.

On the other hand, designers do need to be able to dream big. Anticipate pushback from the engineers. If you want to build something extremely fluid and easy that's a beautiful experience for the user, it probably will mean a lot of work for the developer to build it. That's okay. In fact, it's usually much better than letting the developer drive the design process; usually, they'll match the interface to the database design. (The result is usually not pretty.) As Steve Jobs once said,

> You've got to start with the customer experience and work back toward the technology—not the other way around.

Like everything else in business, you'll likely do a lot of negotiating during design. When great technological solutions arise, they seem like magic to most people who don't realize what's gone on behind the scenes. British science fiction writer Arthur C. Clarke formulated three adages that are known as Clarke's three laws. One of them states, "Any sufficiently advanced technology is indistinguishable from magic."

FINDING YOUR FIELD

This chapter has been all about discovering your users, getting to know them, and delivering them a fantastic experience. As you grow, you'll keep doing that, but keep in mind, you can't be all things to all people. One thing that made Proposify work so well was that we went after an audience we knew intimately, even when people warned us against limiting ourselves and investors advised us to broaden our audience and hire a huge sales team to go after a bigger market.

We knew that we could do that later on but we also understood we needed to own the market we were working in. We learned that from trying to be too many things to too many people at Headspace, where we tried to build websites for everybody and their dog. (And we all know how that story turned out.) The next chapter will focus on how we raised money from investors to grow Proposify.

CHAPTER NINE

FUELLING THE ROCKET SHIP

After Kevin and I went through the horrific experience of trying to sell our agency, and after being turned down countless times by venture capitalists when trying to raise money for Proposify, we decided we never wanted to be at someone else's mercy again. We felt lucky to raise $250,000 from Innovacorp in 2014, and even luckier to not have had to raise again.

Our attention to good design and customer experience paid off. By mid-2015, we had $25,000 in monthly revenue, up from $1,000 the year before. We were getting a good reputation in the startup community, with people saying things to us like "Wow! I hear Proposify's really killing it."

"Raise when you don't need the money. It will be harder to raise later if your growth stagnates," seemed to be the prevailing wisdom from people in the startup community. We started talking to a local group of VCs called Build Ventures. One conversation led to another, and after some initial due diligence, they offered us a term sheet for $1.5 million. The deal was they would take about 21 percent of the company, which would have put us around a $7 million valuation. We balked a little bit about giving up that much of the company for only $1.5 million. (How times had changed; I had struggled to even pay my rent a year earlier!)

In the end, we turned away from the offer.

RISKS OF FUNDRAISING

As it turned out, we didn't really need the money. We were already doing what we wanted to do. We had already begun growing the team, hiring Jennifer Faulkner for marketing, Ricky for product work, a customer support rep, and another developer. What would the money actually change? The truth was, we didn't have a big need to dump money anywhere to scale revenue. Taking the VC offer would have meant taking on $1.5 million that we didn't actually need, while giving up control and diluting ownership in the company.

Turning down the offer was a bit of a gamble. What if our growth stagnated and we began to struggle? We decided it was worth the risk and focused on growth and increasing our revenue every month. We reinvested any profit in hiring more people.

Besides, I had read horror stories of founders losing control of their companies after raising a lot of money very quickly. The founders got removed by their boards or the company was sold for less than its last round's valuation, and investors who had preferred shares got everything while the founders walked away with nothing. Like I said, we learned from our Peter and Jim experience and didn't want to be at anyone else's mercy again.

It was the right decision. In 2016, we celebrated $100,000 in MRR. We'd gotten to that the old-school way, investing profits into growth rather than raising investment dollars.

Don't get sucked into the TechCrunch hysteria; most startups don't have to raise tens or hundreds of millions of dollars to succeed. A lot of great SaaS companies quietly bootstrap their way, building sustainable businesses without the need for venture capital. One example is Mailchimp. In 2016, they made over $400 million with just 550 employees, and they've never raised any investment capital. It's entirely possible.

REASONS TO FUNDRAISE

By the end of 2017, we were at almost $4 million in annual recurring revenue. We had more than doubled our revenue in 2016 and 2017. It was a beautiful thing, but we began wondering what we would ultimately do with the company.

Proposal software is a hot product category in SaaS. Octiv and Qvidian, enterprise competitors in our space, got acquired in recent years by Conga and Upland, respectively. In 2018, SpringCM was acquired by DocuSign for $220 million. Our competitors, Qwilr and PandaDoc, have both raised major rounds of VC cash. We had established ourselves as a front-runner in the market but we knew that competition was only going to get fiercer. We didn't need money to survive now, but we knew the responsible thing to do for our investors, employees, and ourselves was to future-proof the business and start scaling product and sales ahead of revenue.

It sounds hypocritical after everything I've said about risk and giving away control, but we started thinking about financing again, though in a different light.

First of all, I read Tony Robbins's book *Unshakeable* and learned the basics of finance management, which I had never learned before. I learned about inflation, diversification, and portfolio rebalancing; the difference between a hedge fund, an index fund, and a mutual fund; the difference between a bear market and a bull market; and to be greedy when others are fearful, but fearful when others are greedy. I lent the book to Kevin and he read it, too.

Then he called in his friend Richard Alderman, a certified financial planner and adviser at Assante Capital Management, who sat down and offered some advice to Kevin and me. He got us to look at it this way: Proposify was our "high risk" investment, and 100 percent of our net worth was tied to it. The wise course of action would be to pull out some capital from it to reinvest in safer bets, like a diversified, low-risk portfolio that would yield long-term gains. It was pretty much everything that I learned in Tony Robbins's book. But how could we pull cash out of the business? As a VC-funded startup, we would certainly require board approval, and either way, it would cause tax complications if we pulled money out as a dividend, since we were claiming a loss.[14]

Then, I read a story by David Heinemeier Hansson, the cofounder of Basecamp, where he talked about how they took Jeff Bezos's money several years before and explained why. Like us, Fried and Hansson had been proponents of bootstrapping and were very anti-Silicon

---

14 Since we were reinvesting profits into growth, we purposely didn't show profit most years running Proposify. This also meant we were able to save on year-end corporate taxes.

Valley and anti-VC money, but they thought Jeff Bezos was a good guy to have in their corner. Having access to him, his advice, and his network had to be helpful. But also, they didn't *need* his money. Basecamp is a very profitable, successful SaaS company. They weren't trying to grow into the next Salesforce. What the founders wanted was some liquidity. So instead of diluting the company or shares, they sold a portion of their own shares directly to Bezos. In turn, he owned some shares in Basecamp. The transaction de-risked them and gave them a payoff now, so that they could feel very comfortable running Basecamp for the next twenty years. One quote from the article that stuck with us was this:

> It's a shame that arrangements like this aren't more common. I think many companies would be better off if the founders got to hedge their bet just enough to dare go the distance without the anchor of traditional venture capital. The big financial cliff for most entrepreneurs is the difference between no net worth and a few million. The difference between having a few million and a lot of millions is vanishingly small in comparison.

Reading that opened our eyes. We had never thought about things that way, but now we began entertaining the idea of liquidity, and Kevin started going out and talking to people.

BACK TO THE VENTURE CAPITAL CONVERSATION

We went back to that same venture capital group that had offered us the $1.5 million early on and said, "Here's what we're thinking of doing..."

We proposed raising $10 million, giving Kevin and myself each $2 million, and using $6 million as capital in the company. To our surprise, they were open to it, on one condition: we had to find another investor to lead, because they couldn't do the whole deal themselves.

So Kevin went out and talked some more and we ended up with a few suitors at the table. We turned some away because they were too much of a pain in the ass. We understand investors need to look at a lot of data to make an informed decision, but it sometimes seemed like they were overanalyzing spreadsheets instead of looking at the big picture of who we are and where we're going. We wanted an investor who could look at the market, the vision, and the opportunity and get on board with us as partners—not get hung up on a churn cohort from two years ago.

In September of 2017, we met our first serious prospect, Donald (name has been changed), the founder of a new fund based out of San Francisco, who happened to reach out to Kevin while they were both in Boston for HubSpot's Inbound conference. Donald had a decade of experience in a large Silicon Valley-based VC firm (think Instagram, Airbnb, Dropbox, etc.) and really understood what we were doing. He was actively looking for a company in our category to invest in, and we were his top pick. We shared a lot of the same product philosophy. We took it as a good sign when, just days after returning to San Francisco, he flew to Halifax to talk more. He moved fast, which we liked, and got us a term sheet by the end of that week. We felt pretty good about our budding relationship with Donald.

Not long after, we got another strong lead. We connected with a billionaire businessman here in Halifax, John Risley, who expressed interested in us. John, who cofounded Clearwater in the 1970s, now a seafood empire, has invested in several ventures. We weren't sure how it was going to go because he isn't known as a SaaS investor, but we gratefully took the meeting because he's very successful and has been involved with a lot of great companies. It turns out, he actually had been investing in SaaS companies over the last few years. The amount that we were raising was more than John was expecting, so he said he wanted to bring Brendan Paddick—a telecom mogul from Newfoundland and his investment partner—in on the deal. John and Brendan are salt-of-the-earth guys; very real, no-bullshit businessmen.

Meanwhile, much to our surprise, Donald had given us a

term sheet for exactly what we'd asked for. We had two suitors! What to do? We went back to John and Brendan with the offer. They said they'd match it, and with a lot less hassle. Now what?

Kevin and I spent an evening at the office trying to decide whom to go with. Donald would no doubt be a pain in the ass, as a VC from San Francisco, but he was extremely connected in the world of SaaS. John and Brendan were smart, likable guys with significant business experience, but they didn't have the same Silicon Valley connections as Donald. Other than that, it was the same deal in either case.

We opted for Donald, who was intense, as expected, but his energy was exciting. We should have paid attention to some red flags, though, like the feedback I got from a company he'd worked with. They told me Donald was a nightmare to work with, and that if they could have gone back in time, they never would have done a deal with him. I brought it up to Donald, who accused that company of lying on their financials. He was waving more red flags but we were ignoring them.

Frankly, we were too busy fending off Donald's aggressive due diligence. He wanted to see everything and meet with everyone. The meetings should have been cordial but they turned out to be more like interrogations. He came out of them with ideas about who he could fire, not who he could build relationships with. Slowly but surely, I realized he was trying to take control of the company.

When we started the due diligence, Donald told us he was hiring a private investigator to check into our backgrounds. We had nothing to hide, so we agreed to it. About a week before our closing date, Donald pushed us over the edge. Kevin and I jumped on one of our routine weekly calls to discuss the status of the deal. But what Donald said shocked us: "I hate surprises, and my private investigator found out something about you."

Kevin and I were stunned. Kevin joked, "Did I do something on spring break in Fort Lauderdale in 1984 that I don't remember?"

"You guys filed for bankruptcy. You didn't disclose that."

"We didn't file for bankruptcy," I explained. "We filed for a consumer proposal. It's different. And I did disclose that."

He said, "Let's not argue semantics."

I said, "No, it's not semantics. They are literally two different things."

He moved on. "Also, your wife filed a restraining order against you in 2009," he continued.

As soon as he said it, the long-distant memory came back to me. Paula filed for an emergency protection order the first time we separated in 2009 after I had moved out of the house. One day, I was at work and I received a call from the police to meet them so they could deliver the order. No crime was committed and no charges were laid. It just said not to contact her for forty-eight hours. I was mildly annoyed that she had done such a thing. But it was such an insignificant event in my life that it had long ago faded from my mind.

"I remember that. It wasn't really called a restraining order. It was a no-contact order or something."

Donald was incensed. "Do you have any idea what kind of climate we're in right now? What happens when anything like this comes up, especially in Silicon Valley? We have LPs to deal with. They can't find out we're doing business with someone like that."

I was livid. He was accusing me of wrongdoing when nothing of the sort had happened. That was the deal-breaker. He said he needed to think about things, and called Kevin and me up a couple of days later to say we weren't moving ahead. And just like that, one week away from the money hitting our account, it fell through! Maybe he was looking for reasons to back out of the deal. Maybe we weren't what he'd expected. I think the Silicon Valley mentality is growth at all costs—crush and bulldoze people as they get in your way to grow faster. It was just as well we parted ways.

Fortunately, we had kept communications open with John and Brendan, who were more than interested in continuing. It was important to me that we disclose why Donald had backed out, and it wasn't an issue. In mid-January we met with John's investment team, CFFI, to re-pitch the deal. There was back-and-forth over terms, as can be expected, but over the course of several weeks, we were able to come to an agreement everyone was happy with.

One of the terms that changed was that our investors wanted to split up the raise into two tranches. We get half the cash now, and if we hit our revenue goals in a year, we get the second tranche, and they get the shares at the same valuation. If we don't, the investors have the option to not put in the second tranche. It's fair, and it puts pressure on us to hit our targets.

The cash hit our bank accounts in February 2018 when I was down in San Diego for a marketing conference. I had just proposed to Christina, and the next day $1 million was deposited in my bank account. It was a good weekend.

LESSONS FROM FUNDRAISING

We learned quite a few lessons from our fundraising efforts.

1. **Believe in yourself.** It doesn't pay to come to potential investors as supplicants. Instead, as explained by Oren Klaff in his book, *Pitch Anything*, you should do the opposite. Make it seem like *they* are lucky to meet *you*. Assume you can get the money from anywhere. Now it's their job to sell you on why you should take money from them. It sounds cocky and arrogant, and you would think that would turn them off, but it works. I got a sense of this when we were talking to an investor and he expressed doubt that we'd ever hit our revenue milestone. I realized we were starting to lose him, so I pointed out we had two other term sheets on the table and the deal would be closing in a week. If he didn't want in, that would be fine with us. That got his attention. He turned right around, saying, "Oh no, I think this is good." To work this way, you have to be able to separate your emotions from the money. That gives you leverage. You don't seem desperate, like we did with Peter and Jim, who tried to squeeze us. In reality, if you've got a great company and it's growing, investors need you more than you need them. Companies can grow without funding, but investors can't grow their assets without founders and companies. Always treat the deal as though *they* are the ones who would be lucky to get in on it.

2. **Using capital to grow is hard.** When you raise money, there's this belief in the startup world that the cash acts as rocket fuel, but it isn't necessarily true. Cash takes time to spend, and spending it doesn't directly result in growth, at least not right away. Cash isn't a magic bullet. Plenty of startups raise many more millions than we did but still crash and burn. People and processes take time to build. The faster you can scale people and process, the faster revenue growth will catch up. Also, the more you raise, the less room there is for error, and the less you can afford to fuck things up. If like us, you're hesitant to raise, or you're tempted to, I like to think about it like this:
    - Is your product already a leader in its niche?
    - Is your market large and growing?
    - What won't change in ten years?[15]
    - Is competition growing, and are they raising a lot of money and/or getting acquired?
    - Do you know how you'd leverage the capital? What will you change with cash that you can't without the cash?
    - Is your business sustainable without the money? Never raise out of desperation. It'll lead to shit deals.
    - Do you just want money, or do you really believe

---

15 Jeff Bezos said that he can't imagine a world in ten years where customers don't care about low prices and fast delivery times, so he knows to pour resources into those elements of Amazon's offering.

you can 20x your business and do right by your investors?

3. **When you don't make damn sure your values align with a potential investor, things can't possibly go well.** In hindsight, we're really glad things fell apart with Donald. He was the wrong investor for us, whereas John and Brendan's vision and values align with ours. We share a common interest in our community in Atlantic Canada and want to build a world-class company to create jobs here and support our local startup ecosystem. We don't believe in growth at all costs.

4. **So-called smart money is overrated.** Investors can be extremely helpful even though they aren't experts in your niche. You can make up for knowledge gaps by having advisors and coaches outside of your investors. It's also worth noting that Donald had only worked in a large institutional venture capital firm, otherwise he's an armchair entrepreneur, whereas John and Brendan are CEOs who walk the walk and have actually built billion-dollar businesses.

5. **The "raise early and raise often" wisdom doesn't work for everyone.** We've found it's best to stick to growing as fast as you can organically by reinvesting profit. You'll get less dilution and a better valuation when and if you decide to raise later.

6. **Raising money is hard and distracting.** Some founders think they just need to get a yes from an

investor and that's it—cash is in the bank—but the yes is only the beginning. Due diligence is always hell, no matter who it's with.
7. **It's okay not to be the VC-whispering type.** Some entrepreneurs are and that's okay. For whatever reason, Kevin and I have never had much luck with traditional venture capitalists.

Open your mind to the pros of raising money, but stick to your principles throughout your journey. We almost didn't, and it could have meant disaster for us and our business.

THE BEST OF BOTH WORLDS

The deal we struck gives us the best of both worlds. Financially, we have breathing room to work on scaling the business, which is what we want to do. If somebody came along now and offered us $20 million for the company, we could say no. And we have. We're no longer in a desperate situation where we have to make the quickest buck we can.

On a personal level, the money is a huge life-changer. I used some of it to pay off my consumer proposal and car loan. When Christina and I decided to build a house, I was able to buy the land with cash. I put the rest of the money into savings and investments. After so many years of struggling with debt, it feels incredibly good to be financially free. The money doesn't mean I can retire at thirty-five and never work again, but it provides a welcome safety net and lets me build up a nest egg that will grow over time.

The deal did mean we had to give up some control. John and Brendan have seats on the board, and we need to report to them whether we hit our quarterly targets or not. I thought I would hate that but, surprisingly, I find the discipline helps me grow as a founder. Being accountable to the board means I hold myself to a higher standard.

We made an excellent deal, and you can, too. The biggest lesson to take away, though, is that no deal is closed until it's closed. We were a week away from closing when all that shit hit the fan with Donald. Save your celebration for the day that money lands in your account.

CHAPTER TEN

DEMAND

I've shared Proposify's basic trajectory, but if you're an entrepreneur looking to follow in our footsteps, you probably want to know more about the nuts and bolts of making a business like this work, especially from the marketing and sales side. To give you that, we need to go back in time to 2012, when I was still running Headspace.

I designed a website for an app called Pitch Perfect.

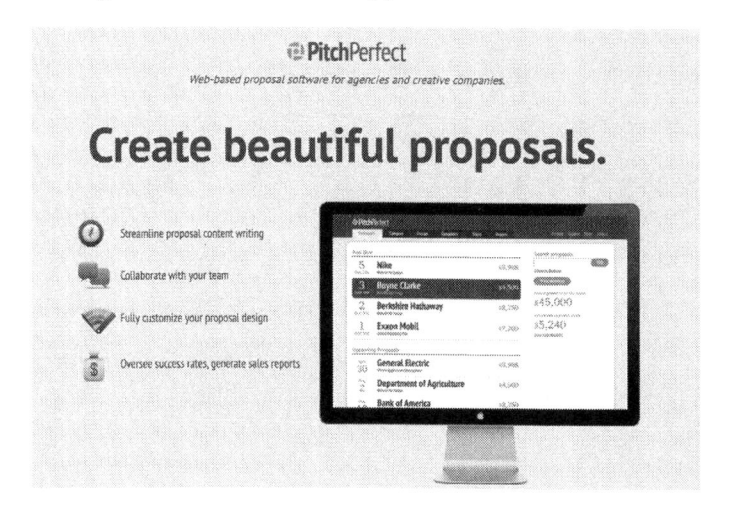

It looks like we had a product, right? We didn't. Visitors to the site were asked to sign up to get an email when we launched, and those signups let us gauge whether anybody was interested in the product at all. Using a small AdWords spend of a couple hundred dollars, I bid on words like "proposal software" and "proposal templates" just to see if anybody was searching for them.

I also did content marketing. I set up a blog and wrote articles about proposals—how to write a proposal, how to write an executive summary, and what goes into a perfect case study. I also contributed articles to other blogs to get a link back, which drove referral traffic, and the links helped boost our organic search traffic. Through that alone we were able to build an initial email list of about a hundred people who said they were interested in the product, so we knew we'd hit on something.

And so, throughout 2013, when we launched our minimum viable product, and the tail end of 2014, when we were beginning to hit product/market fit (under the Proposify name), most of our website traffic was generated through word of mouth, referrals, and search engines. Our traffic climbed from about five thousand monthly visitors in 2014 to forty thousand in 2015. About 5 percent of those visitors would sign up for a free trial of Proposify. As it turned out, the residual benefit of me having a decade of experience building brands and websites, and leveraging digital marketing for my clients, also helped me become adept at doing those same things for my own company.

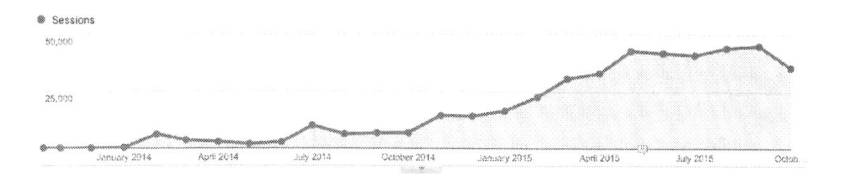

AUDIENCE AND MESSAGING

Nicholas Kusmich speaks at a lot of marketing conferences, and something I heard him once say stood out to me. He said, "Great marketing isn't when you understand your audience; it's when your audience feels understood by you."

I believe that the reason we were consistently able to generate so many leads, even when our product wasn't yet good enough to convert those leads into customers or retain them long term, was because our audience felt understood by us. We weren't selling proposal software to a broad audience across multiple industries at that time, we were selling to owners of small design and marketing agencies. We were selling to ourselves. A lot of my blog posts and headlines acknowledged how hard it is to run a small agency. And I understood as well as they did the rush of closing new business for your agency, of having your proposal accepted. And how bitterly disappointing it felt to have your prospect turn down your proposal. It wasn't just a number on a balance sheet, it was being able to make payroll.

I also wanted Proposify to have a personality. It's important for your customers to not only get use out of your product, but also feel good about using it for more than the utility. After all, your competitors can copy a lot of your product's functionality, but it's hard for them to copy your brand once it's been established. And so, I began putting humour and personality into our website, blog articles, and ad headlines. "Writing proposals sucks. We make it suck less" is a headline I wrote for a Twitter ad years ago that we still use in various places today.

RIGHT-BRAINED MARKETING

No matter what kind of business you're building, you need consistent leads coming into your marketing funnel every week. As time goes on, you need to find ways to grow the amount of leads and also increasingly convert more of them into customers.

If you're not a marketer you can use outbound sales tactics in the early days, like cold-calling and emailing people who might need your product, and for many, founder-led sales get them initial traction. But eventually you're going to need a marketing team who can drive qualified traffic, perhaps in addition to outbound efforts. As we began to rapidly increase our monthly revenue in 2015, I knew that I was going to need help producing more of the content that was driving traffic and leads to us.

Our first hire was Jennifer Faulkner, whom I had worked with at Impact and Modern Media. She'd done copywriting and brand strategy for our clients at Headspace, so Kevin and I knew her work, and we liked her as a person. Plus, she was already very familiar with our brand and was excited to come on board. Jen excels at communication. She is incredible at storytelling, crafting our messaging and unique value proposition, writing ad headlines, video scripts, and anything else that will attract the right people to our product.

What Jen is not good at, and she'll tell you, is technical stuff like analyzing spreadsheets. Her imitation of a programmer writing code is to hold up her two index fingers and mimic typing while making the robotic sound effect, "beep boop boop boop beep." It's funny how broad the term "marketer" really is, because it touches so many different disciplines. You could be a search-engine optimization specialist, a public relations professional, or a copywriter for television commercials, and in any of those scenarios you could rightly call yourself a marketer.

Over the years I began boiling it down to *right-brained*

marketing and *left-brained marketing*. The right side of your brain is supposedly where creativity comes from: music, art, poetry. It's a kaleidoscope of shape and colour—the hippie stoner of the brain. The left side of the brain is the colder, more analytical, black-and-white part of the brain—the more prudent, sensible older sibling who reminds the right side it's time to leave in order to make curfew. It takes both sides to function properly.

It's no different in marketing; You need people on your team who can analyze data, run growth experiments, drive down your cost per lead, and put automation into place. Those are great people to have on board. But they are rarely the same people who can craft a compelling message that resonates, or design a gorgeous visual that stands out in somebody's Facebook feed. The two sides need each other to be successful. First, let's discuss the different jobs your right-brained marketers will do.

CONTENT MARKETING

Everybody knows they need to exercise to be healthy. Some people actually do it, while others spend more time thinking about it than actually going to the gym. They'll spend hours downloading workout apps, reading blogs, or shopping for the best workout gear but then stay home and do nothing. The ones who've got the results are the ones who've put in the work consistently for years.

It's the same with content. You can't just think about it; you can't plan it; you have to *just do it*. (Side note: What a great tagline. I wonder if it's taken?) If you do it poorly at first, that's fine; you can't learn to surf without falling in the water a few times. You'll get it.

Then, like working out, you have to do it again. And again. Doing it once will get zero results. It's only through regular, consistent practice that you'll make progress. It might take a year or two to build up your content, but once you have a catalogue of content out in the universe, the effect can be massive. We had over a million unique visitors to our website last year, and we're far from being one of the biggest sites in the world. That started with content we published three or four years ago.

Unlike paid advertising, where as soon as you stop paying for it you no longer get to enjoy the benefit, content is evergreen. You pay once to create it, but then it can bring you customers for the next ten years. The thing I love about content is that it compounds, like recurring revenue. One blog post alone might not generate a lot of traffic, but over time, you might have hundreds of articles each appearing in search engines for terms like "when should you hire HR" or "how to create a sales process." As that search traffic accumulates across your whole site you'll be able to convert thousands of customers into leads and eventually buyers. Of course, your content has to be good to stand out.

So how do you create great content?

The thing that holds a lot of entrepreneurs back from blogging is imposter syndrome. They feel like they aren't experts and don't have anything unique or compelling to share. You might be surprised to learn that I still feel this way whenever I put out a new piece of content. In fact, I'm feeling it right now as I write the book you're currently holding in your hands!

The thing is, you don't have to be an expert to write compelling business content. If you simply document your journey and share tactical examples of how you applied different strategies, a certain audience of people will engage with the story. A help desk software company called Groove nailed this. Their founder, Alex Turnbull, wrote that their startup was still in its early days, but every week he wanted to share what they were trying and explain what was working and what wasn't. He called it the *Journey to 100k* blog. Every week, he posted numbers reflecting his progress. People loved it. They checked back every week to see how it was going. This is the approach I take with every piece of content I create.

You may think your company is too small to make this

work but it's probably not. In fact, when you're small and new, your story has an authentic feel to it that people love. They're drawn to the reality of someone saying, "I've got three customers and here's how I'm going to get my fourth." Content marketing is more competitive than ever, and it's only going to get more so. The more authentic you are, the more you'll stand out. And the more regular you are with publishing content, the better you'll get at the craft.

AUDIO AND VIDEO

You don't have to be a great writer to be a great content marketer. Some find it easier to share their thoughts using their face, voice, or through the use of visuals. Gary Vaynerchuk comes to mind here. Most of the content he produces is based on keynotes he delivers at conferences, guest interviews that he does, audience Q&As, and having his camera guy follow him around as he pontificates in the back of an Uber. His team turns all of those rants into content across a variety of media, including books, podcast episodes, blog articles, Instagram images, and YouTube videos. "Gary Vee" has the personality, the charisma, and the gift of gab to be the best in the world at it.

Video and podcasts are media that are on the rise and only getting more popular. Writing is still as relevant as ever, but there's something about being able to literally talk into someone's ear as they're out for a run or commuting to work that builds rapport in a way that written articles can't.

In February of 2013, Kevin and I started a podcast called *Agencies Drinking Beer*, modelled after Jerry Seinfeld's television show *Comedians in Cars Getting Coffee*. On the show, I interviewed agency owners who were in the trenches, day to day. It was meant to feel like sharing stories over a beer at the pub. The show resonated well with our target audience, allowed us to gather fresh content from other people, and provided another channel to ensure our audience felt heard. For a while, Kevin and I actually did drink beer while we were recording, and our guests did, too. Even if they lived in Australia and it was eight in the morning in their time zone, you'd hear them crack open their beer and proudly announce they were on *Agencies Drinking Beer*. On a few occasions, we had one too many and the quality of the content left a little to be desired, so we decided to give our livers a break and rebranded the podcast.

One of the biggest benefits of podcasting is that it helps build your network. You can reach out to an expert in your industry and ask them to be a guest on your podcast. Many will accept your invitation in order to boost their own popularity (and ego), and in turn, you'll be able to build relationships with influencers. I've been able to talk to incredible guests over the years with thousands of social media followers, some of whom I now call friends, simply by hosting a podcast.

As of this writing, I've veered away from guest interviews and I work primarily on creating videos for YouTube that also get turned into podcast episodes and written articles. There's substantially less competition for B2B content on YouTube and it lets your fans put a face to your voice. In fact, a video I released about cold email ranks at the top of YouTube search results for the term "cold email" and has gotten over thirty thousand views as of this writing. It also, in turn, converted 161 users to sign up for a free trial and converted twenty-four paying customers this year. Twenty-four customers might not seem like a lot, but that's only counting direct conversions from this one post. And we have hundreds of posts.

BRAND

Content builds context, and brand rises from that context. Nike is not just the "swoosh." It's everything around the brand: the pride in feeling like an athlete when you wear Nike. Every piece of collateral you see around Nike is just enhancing and strengthening that image.

It all starts with a name, something we struggled with for

a while. I got the idea for the name Proposify around 2013, but before that, I thought of it as Pitch Perfect. The trouble was, people associated the name with either music software or pitch deck software. We might have persevered, but when the Anna Kendrick movie of the same name came out, we moved on. How could we compete with an a cappella girls' group?

We concentrated on the proposals themselves when we chose our name, and I'll be the first one to say it: Proposify is not a great name. People see it written and struggle to pronounce it. I feel like I need to place the phonetic pronunciation (pru·POH·sif·I) next to it sometimes. But it tells our story. (And we're not alone. Google is a pretty goofy name, too. And Apple has nothing to do with sleek sophistication and well-designed technology. It's a fruit.) But once your name becomes associated with your brand values, whether it's easy-to-use software, friendly customer support, or powerful technology, it doesn't really matter what your name is.

We usually think of brand as outward-facing—it's how we're perceived by people outside the company. But branding can't be a facade; it has to come from within. I wanted our company culture to influence our brand, even when there were only three of us in the company. We understood that a culture would evolve naturally, with or without our input, as more employees came on board, so we needed to think about how to guide that evolution.

It started with hiring. As I mentioned earlier in the chapter, I always wanted our brand to be lighthearted and humorous. So we used humour as a litmus test to judge whether somebody was a good fit. If our website and copy was going to be down-to-earth, natural, and humorous, we obviously had to hire people who were that way as well. Our culture would drive our work and our brand. It's why today our customer support reps are actively encouraged to joke around with customers and make them laugh. It's who we are. When a new customer support rep comes from a big bank or insurance company where they're supposed to stick to the corporate script, they're always surprised when we encourage them to joke around with customers or post funny gifs in chat. It usually takes them a little bit of time to get used to that but they come to love it.

In 2015, we performed an exercise to develop a clear vision for our company. Jen's suggestion years ago, I had read Clotaire Rapaille's book *The Culture Code* and was taken by the idea that a brand strategy could be boiled down to one word—the company's "culture code," a code that captures the spirit of the business. For example, Jeep's culture code is "horse" because Jeep taps into the adventurous spirit of riding a horse on the wild frontier (it's apparently why Jeep has round headlights—they look like eyes). The American president's culture code is "Moses" because unlike most other Western nations, whose politics are boring by comparison, America often elects presidents who seemingly rise up from among the common people to implement bold changes and lead them to the promised land. Whether or not you agree with Rapaille's conclusions, he offers an interesting way to look at branding.

I wanted to figure out what our culture code was, so Jen took the whole company through the exercise. When she finished, she had realized the culture code for Proposify: Q.

Yes, Q. It was perfect. Just like Q in the James Bond movies, we worked behind the scenes with all the cool toys. We did it with a little banter and a constant battle of wits. James Bond might go out and fulfill the missions but we provided all the tools he needed. Sometimes Bond doesn't quite know how to use the exploding pen properly and the car is usually totalled by the end but he gets the job done.

We only use this code internally. We think of our customers as James Bond—they're on a mission to close the deal. We're just giving them the tools and help to do it.

LEFT-BRAINED MARKETING

Jennifer was amazing with all of the right-brained marketing covered above but we needed more. We needed answers to questions like: How many leads are coming in the door? How many can we convert? How many leave at the end of the day? How long can we keep a customer?

Having the skills to answer those questions makes all the difference when you try to scale the company. We needed someone to pay attention to the more left-brained, scientific side of marketing, things like managing a Facebook ad spend, or conducting A/B testing on a landing page, or analyzing Google Analytics reports.

Because it's rare to find one person who excels on both sides, I decided to hire somebody who was more of a "growth hacker" to work with Jennifer.

The job ad said exactly that: we were looking for a "growth hacker." Most people didn't know what that meant, which was fine with us. I named the position that way to weed out the bad fits. I was amused and delighted when someone who is a growth manager at Yahoo! applied for the position. He lived in San Francisco and was looking to make a move. He flew up to Halifax on his own dime, and Kevin and I showed him around town. In the end, he was making $450,000 at his current job, which was almost what our last year's revenue was, so we passed. Furthermore, I don't believe hiring someone who is effective at a big company necessarily translates to success at a startup where resources are limited and there's more of a JFDI (just fucking do it) culture.

I kept looking at applicants. Eventually, I came across Patrick Edmonds. He was young, in his mid-twenties, and ran digital advertising for a PR agency in town. He was very upfront about what he was well read up about but didn't have hands-on experience actually doing. When I interviewed him, I asked him to articulate a growth experiment he'd been in, including his original hypothesis, what he used as the criteria for testing it, and how he knew whether he had attained the statistical significance necessary to deem it a success or a failure. He nailed it.

We brought him on board in 2016, and he was the missing piece of the puzzle. I remember Ben Yoskovitz, one of our board members, once asking me to break down all of our metrics segmented by plan size. I was completely dumbfounded on how to do this. I asked Patrick and the file was sent to me within twenty minutes. Another time, Patrick came to me and said, "Hey, I know you extended your free trials from fourteen days to thirty days last year. I looked at six months of data, and your conversion was actually better at fourteen days." We switched back and our conversion increased. After a year, I promoted Patrick to CMO. It was a big step up, but I believed then, and still believe, that he has the skills, attitude, and aptitude to excel in the role.

SEARCH ENGINE OPTIMIZATION

Historically, SEO has been our primary avenue for traffic. People search Google for proposal templates, how to write a proposal, and proposal software.

To get even more people looking for us, we used some other tactics, like comparing ourselves to the competition in articles that described us both and gave us the opportunity to mention our features. After that, people looking for an alternative to our competitors could find us with a simple search: "Quote Roller alternative." In the early days, when we had no traffic, I also commented on reviews of competitors' products, with a quick, "Hey, this product looks great. There's this other really cool one I found, too, that gives you a lot of design flexibility. It's called Proposify. Check them out!" I never slammed the competitor, just let potential customers know we were out there, too.

If you have a great product, you can eventually stop doing some of those early growth hacks; the product will naturally generate word-of-mouth recommendations. After you've hit product/market fit, you'll do even less. When people start typing your brand name directly into their browser's URL bar, you know they're finding you by word of mouth. You've arrived.

ADVERTISING

Digital advertising is one of the most foolproof ways to drive traffic to your website. That said, much like other marketing channels, it requires skill and experience to execute effectively. Where most newbies starting off go wrong is with bad targeting; they pay too much money to drive bad leads into their funnel who don't convert. I knew that managing AdWords and Facebook ad spends was a weakness of mine, and it's why, other than a few experiments, I decided to outsource it until I had the talent in-house to manage it.

One of the more surprising things I learned as we increased our monthly spend on digital advertising was how creative you can get with how you deploy your ad dollars. For example, you don't have to waste money trying to drive cold traffic (people who have never heard of you) to your website. We already had a lot of visitors because of our strong organic traffic. Instead, we retargeted the people who already visited our website and signed up for a trial but didn't log back in to the product. Patrick used Facebook ads to entice people to download our free Proposify iPhone app. Those people were statistically more likely to then upgrade to a paid account. Why? It was just a companion app, not the full product. Our theory is that users who installed the mobile app felt like Proposify was now embedded in their lives. It was an ingenious way to use advertising to drive sales, not just traffic.

OTHER LEFT-BRAINED MARKETING ACTIVITIES

You can break down left-brained marketing into multiple strategies, tactics, and disciplines.

- **Data and analytics.** Believe it or not, large software companies like Shopify and Uber have entire departments just dedicated to data. You need to be able to accurately track activity in your website and product, analyze it, and marry the data across dozens of applications, like your CRM, help desk, and product dashboard, and use the data to make better decisions. This becomes more complicated the bigger you get and the more users you have.
- **Marketing automation.** As your user base grows it becomes impractical to have a human manually monitor everyone's activity and send the right messages in the right channels to the right person at the right time. In a nutshell, that's what marketing automation is all about.
- **Conversion optimization.** Have you ever been to a website and, after a few seconds, closed the browser tab because it wasn't what you were looking for?

That's how the majority of people behave on websites. In fact, if only 5 percent of the people who land on a website sign up for an offer or make a purchase, that's generally considered good conversion! To increase your conversion at different stages of your marketing funnel you need to work to understand where people may be getting hung up and come up with a hypothesis for how to fix it. It might be a change to your headline, an image, or the colour of the background. Then you run a test so that 50 percent of new visitors see the original version (control) and 50 percent see the version with the new changes (variation). At the end of the experiment, you'll learn whether or not those changes really did make a difference and more visitors in the variation converted, so you can roll it across the entire website. That's a very simple explanation of what CRO is, but again, it requires a left-brained, data-driven mindset, compared to just arbitrarily throwing ideas at the wall to see what sticks.

SUMMARY

This chapter has outlined some of the various marketing activities my team and I performed building Proposify. If it sounds daunting, it's because it is! But if you want to be a successful entrepreneur you're going to need to get good at marketing. In fact, I believe sales and marketing, the ability to find paying customers, is one of the most—

if not the most—necessary factor in being successful in business. But as you may have noticed reading, I'm not an expert in any of the disciplines I described. I'm good at some, competent in others, and awful at the rest. As of this writing, our marketing team at Proposify consists of two designers, three writers, one community manager, and two analytics and automation specialists, all led by Patrick and Jen. As a founder, I don't have to be the best because, as long as I know what greatness looks like, I can hire other people to make up for my own weaknesses.

CHAPTER ELEVEN

GROWTH

Have you ever tried to balance yourself on a bicycle when it wasn't moving? I know some people can, but if you're like me, you fall over. What about if you are cycling up a hill and then stop pedalling? First you slow down, then you stop, then you begin rolling backwards, and in a few seconds you're on your ass.

Business is a lot like that, too. Starting a business is kind of like getting on a bike and pedalling up a hill—it takes a lot of work and gravity isn't on your side. But with enough time and effort you can begin climbing the hill and make it to the point where sustaining the forward momentum becomes easier. Never easy, but easier. But then if something else happens, some external force interferes with you, like a market crash or stiff competition, or you simply get tired and stop pedalling, the business never stays where it's at; it always falls backwards. Growing your business isn't about greed; it's about survival. If you're not growing, you're dying.

Growth is so important that it's the primary metric with which most companies are valued. For better or worse, a startup that is burning cash with no hope of generating any retained earnings for shareholders but is rapidly growing its top-line revenue or user base can be blessed with astonishing valuations from investors. It's why behemoths like Amazon, Facebook, and Google continue eating up the world, acquiring companies, decimating competitors, and moving into new markets. I'm not saying it's right, or that it won't cause the stock market to crash, but unfortunately, it's the way capitalism tends to work. If you're an entrepreneur, this is the game you're playing. And the name of the game is Growth.

LEVERS

When most people think about growth, they tend to think it involves mainly acquisition, driving an ever-increasing army of buyers to your website. And building a great marketing team, like I described in the previous chapter, certainly does that. But one of the more surprising aspects of running a business that I've learned is that *acquisition is not the most important factor in growing your recurring revenue*. What do I mean?

Let's break out growth levers into three categories: acquisition, monetization, and retention.

- **Acquisition** is getting new customers in the door.
- **Monetization** is the amount of money your customers pay you.
- **Retention** is keeping your customers from leaving you.

What would happen if you were to improve each of those growth levers by 1 percent? Would each of them equally grow your bottom line? The data suggests no. SaaS pricing experts Price Intelligently conducted a study and found that increasing each lever by 1 percent would grow the bottom line at different rates. Here's what would happen:

- **Acquisition**: 3.32 percent
- **Monetization**: 12.70 percent
- **Retention**: 6.71 percent

Acquisition is dead last! This proves that if you kept your growth of new customers flat but increased the amount they paid and were able to keep more of them around, you would grow much faster than if you just worked on getting new customers in the door.

ACQUISITION

Remember how much I struggled running an agency? It was because our clients didn't pay us enough money, and after most projects we needed to hustle to find the next client. We weren't able to keep clients with us and have them gradually pay us more money over time. Thus, we needed to put more time, effort, and money into writing proposals to win over new clients.

To understand how to improve monetization and retention, you first have to know your customer acquisition cost (CAC) to lifetime value (LTV) ratio: how much you're spending to acquire a new customer versus how much revenue that customer generates for you over the course of their lifetime with your business.

If you're spending $20,000 in sales and marketing every month to get ten new customers, each of those customers cost you $2,000. You have a CAC of $2,000.

Next, compare that with how much a customer brings in over their lifetime: their lifetime value, or LTV. If they only make one $1,000 purchase and never come back, you're losing a lot of money. It's true that, in the beginning, you might have to spend more per customer just to get people in. As the company grows, though, you need to get more from each customer.

Starbucks, for instance, has an LTV of about $20,000. On average, that's how much a customer will pay Starbucks over the course of their life. If Starbucks knows how much each customer is worth, they know how much they can afford to spend on advertising and marketing.

You wouldn't expect that each customer would pay back their acquisition cost in the first month but, over time, they should be paying you back many times more what it cost you to get them in the first place. This is called the payback period. You ideally want this to be as short as possible, because it's better to get paid back within a few months rather than a few years.

Here's how it relates to monetization and retention: the more revenue you can extract from a customer, the more you can afford to invest in sales and marketing, and the shorter your payback period will be. And the longer you can keep them as a customer, the more profit you'll be able to generate after the payback period. Make sense?

MONETIZATION

When we started selling Proposify, we looked at how other SaaS companies handled pricing and followed suit. We saw companies like Groove charging fifteen dollars per user, per month, so we used that as a baseline.

That was a fine start but we couldn't leave that price static as we grew. We had to revisit that decision over time, measure how we were doing, and try some experiments to see if we could do better. The goal is to strike a balance between charging so much that a customer reconsiders their investment and so little that they doubt the value of the product. You don't want to be leaving money on the table.

PRICE BASED ON VALUE

A beginner's mistake many new entrepreneurs make is to price their product or service based on how much it cost them to make. A glass of lemonade costs five cents to make, so we'll sell it for twenty-five cents. Seventy-five percent gross margin—not bad, right? But what if you were selling it in the desert? I once visited New York and walked across the Brooklyn Bridge. There were merchants selling water for five dollars—more than I'd ever pay for a bottle of water in a store. But right there and then? It was hot and I was thirsty. It was a "shut up and take my money" moment.

My point is, *customers don't care about how much it costs you, they care about the value it offers them.* If a product that costs you $1,000 to make but makes them $1 million per year and costs them $100,000 to buy, they'll tell you to shut up and take their money.

So how do you quantify the value you create for your customers?

To get to that number, you have to know your value metric. Some also call it a North Star metric. It's the thing that, as your customers use more, the more value they receive from your product. For an analytics company, it might be the amount of data a customer uses. When you first install the script from your website to start tracking visitors, it's free. As you get more visitors and people start using your product, the price goes up. Dropbox did that with file storage; the more data you store with them, the more expensive it becomes. That's a natural value metric.

For social media companies like Facebook, it's daily active users. The more people log on to Facebook every day, the more data they share about themselves, and the more data they can sell to advertisers (like you).

If you're running a service business, you might be tempted to charge by the hour, like we did at Headspace. Almost every service business starts here because it's the easiest value metric to use. Take it from me: that's a huge mistake. Customers don't care how much time you spend on something. They just want to know if it's worth it.

More agencies have moved to value-based pricing. Instead of telling the customer how long a project will take, they'll say, "We're doing this marketing activity. Our goal is to get you from a thousand qualified leads a month to ten thousand." The customer will do the math and say, "Wow, if I had ten times the amount of leads, I could do this much more in revenue. That'll make me $1 million a month. This is worth it!"

A common approach is to charge 10 percent of the value you bring to your customers. Generally, they're going to be fine with that. Then, it's up to you to follow through and deliver that value.

We always struggle with our value metric at Proposify. Early on, we charged a flat fee per user, per month. That pricing model didn't work very well, partly because the product was still new. Our early adopters were used to trying out new, unproven, and buggy products, and they generally wouldn't want to pay more to add an additional user. If they wanted someone else to use it, they'd just share the password.

We were also marketing to very small companies. We started to realize there was a big difference between companies that only wrote five proposals a month and companies that had several teams writing fifty proposals a month. Those high-volume teams were willing to pay more, which meant it made sense to bucket our pricing into tiers.

We've had modest success with this approach, but have discovered there are certain limits to usage-based pricing. It turns out that the bigger companies, the ones who can pay more, don't actually put as much value on the number of proposals they write. They put more value on the team itself and how many people they have using it, so we have gone back to seat-based pricing. But, more importantly, we found that add-on features are the real value driver.

The experiment is ongoing for us, and it should be for you, too. Don't just set it and forget it—you should be running a pricing test every quarter. Iterate, learn, then iterate some more.

> **CONSIDERING FREEMIUM?**
>
> All this talk about numbers, but there's one we haven't mentioned: zero. Should you ever give anything away for free? A lot of people in SaaS think so; they have seen the success of products like Dropbox using the "freemium" model. Freemium does work—it can drive an insane number of users to your product. If you try it, just realize freemium is more of a marketing play than a pricing play, and be sure to have to an upgrade strategy, so that, over time, a good percentage of your customers won't be able to keep getting value without upgrading to a paid plan.
>
> That said, freemium works for only a small percentage of SaaS companies. We tried it back in 2006. I was totally on board, even after hearing all the arguments for and against. I thought it was the way to go to drive growth and traffic. Some of our teammates were skeptical, Kevin included, but we tried it. For about a month.
>
> When we put out freemium, we thought our paid plans would continue on their current trajectory, but that we'd add more customers through freemium. Instead, our paying subscribers levelled off. Before the free option, we were growing at 10 percent month over month, but it went to 1 percent as soon as we launched the free plan. We did add about five thousand free users within a week, so maybe it would have played out long term; but at the time, we hadn't raised any money and were still trying to build enough of a profit to keep hiring people. Maybe we'll experiment again one day.

[Handwritten margin note: freemium can cannibalize users from a paid plan]

SEGMENT YOUR CUSTOMERS

Sometimes you have all the numbers you need, but you have to look at them from a new perspective. When we compared lifetime value and churn by segment and compared mid-tier pricing to high-end pricing, we noticed

↑ *loss aversion*

that <u>churn went down exponentially as the price went up, thus lifetime value was going up.</u>

Most people think the more you charge, the bigger the risk that you'll lose a customer, but we were charging more and they were sticking around longer. It was fascinating to see that once somebody pays into your higher-tier pricing, they'll rarely leave. <mark>On the low-tier pricing, customers drop out much faster.</mark> By doing segmentation, we realized we don't want to focus on this end of the market at all.

Customers in each tier share certain attributes, but you can also break each tier down into different personas. If you serve everyone from freelancers to small businesses to enterprise, you could set a price tier for each category of client. The tiers should be simple and straightforward, and obvious to someone who visits your website and looks at your pricing package. They should be able to see that they fall naturally into one of your tiers.

<u>Avoid creating a pricing page with eight different plans, each with massive lists breaking down every single feature.</u> That's too much for the customer to take in. Keep it simple, let the customer recognize themselves in one of your plans, and they'll check it out.

SALES

You may be thinking, after reading this, that the only way to go is up; sell higher-priced products and services to bigger companies that have got the money to pay. In a sense, yes, but remember there's always a trade-off.

When you sell higher-priced products to higher-end clients, you'll almost always need a higher-touch sales model. A VP of finance at a Fortune 1000 enterprise is not going to sign up for a free trial and then add her credit card at the end for a six-figure annual fee. In fact, they may never even know your product exists at all unless someone calls them up to cold pitch the solution. It might require three product demos to three different departments in the company, seven follow-up calls, and redlining a service-level agreement between your lawyer and their legal team over six months to ever land the deal.

You're probably going to need a sales team made up of BDRs (business development reps) to do the prospecting and qualifying and hand over sales-qualified leads to account executives who handle demoing and closing. You'll need your own VP of sales. You'll need to pay out commission. Sales cycles might take twelve months. But since every customer will be worth a lot more money, you can afford it, and after all that effort, the customer will probably never churn. The bottom line is that moving up-market has its own challenges, but who said building a business would be easy?

RETENTION AND EXPANSION

Churn—the rate at which customers cancel their subscriptions—is the bane of all SaaS businesses' existence. Keeping customers around pays high dividends; your revenue will compound each month if you do this well. If you start losing customers, however, the numbers go downhill fast. If, for example, you lose 5 percent of your customers every month, you'll lose 60 percent of your customers in a year. If you haven't kept acquiring new customers over the year, you'll be left with only 40 percent of your base. That's why churn is such a scary word in SaaS. There's no point paying to add water to a leaky bucket, especially when water is scarce. No market is infinite, so you could theoretically run out of customers one day.

As you grow, churn has a bigger impact on your business. As I already mentioned, churn tends to be higher when you sell to small businesses. They go out of business at a higher rate, their credit cards are more likely to get declined, or they simply abandon your product because they found something cheaper. And remember, if customers are cancelling after only a few months, they may never pay back their acquisition cost, let alone generate profit for the business.

So what can you do about churn?

FIND OUT WHY THEY LEAVE

One way to find out why people leave is exit surveys. We've used these consistently—to cancel their account, customers have to finish a quick survey. It's a multiple-choice survey, where we ask, "What caused you to cancel your account?" Notice we don't blame the user or accuse them of anything, we blame ourselves. Obviously, we didn't offer enough value or demonstrate it effectively. I want to know how we could have done better.

Answer choices include "I don't have proposals to write," "I had problems using your product," or "I'm switching to a competitor." At the next level, we ask a few more detailed questions, like, "If you're leaving for a competitor, which competitor is it?" We want to know who's siphoning away our customers. If we know why customers are leaving, we can uncover trends and do whatever is in our power to improve things for the next cohort of customers.

Sometimes there's nothing you can do. The answers to these surveys helped us figure out that customers on the low-tier pricing usually leave because they don't want to keep paying for a product during periods when they don't have proposals to write. That's what gave us the impetus to focus more on upstream, mid-level companies who always have a need for our product. Some SaaS businesses can sell to consumers because most of us are going to keep our ten-dollar Netflix subscription even if we go a month without watching a movie. For Proposify, it's not like that. We can't build a big business out of tiny customers. Neither can Salesforce, Box, or Marketo, for that matter, which is why they focus on mid-market and enterprise customers.

ONBOARDING AND ACTIVATION

Sometimes it isn't that your product doesn't offer value, it's just that you do a lousy job of demonstrating it, so users never get activated in the first place. The cardinal sin most new SaaS products commit is the empty dashboard dump. It's after you create a new account as a user and the first thing you see when you log in is an empty dashboard. There's no walkthrough, no first step the app encourages you to take. Of course you're going to bounce.

At Proposify, we regularly work to improve user onboarding: taking the user on a journey from getting interested in the product, to using it, to actually getting value from it.

Experiment with your onboarding approach. Try creating a new account every couple of months and see what your customer sees. When they enter their email address to sign up for your free trial, what happens next? Are they dumped onto an empty dashboard with no clues about what to do? That could be why you're seeing a lot of people just logging out and never coming back. Now you know what to fix.

Your goal in onboarding is to get the user far enough in that they experience an initial burst of success from using the product. With an email marketing tool, for instance, the customer gets that first hit of dopamine when they send content out to their list for the first time. That's the actual activation. They've used the product. They didn't just sign up then bounce and never come back. For an analytics tool, it might be once they install the tracking script on their website and begin seeing data in their account.

Effective onboarding that leads to activation is crucial but not easy. At Proposify, we're constantly asking how we can bridge the gap between people being interested in our product to making Proposify part of their everyday life. We're glad they love the free template they get when they sign up, but we want to know what keeps them coming back to us. What makes it more of a sixty- to ninety-day activation campaign than just a fourteen-day free trial? There are no easy answers; onboarding is just another area where you have to keep experimenting to figure out what works best for you and your company.

Believe it or not, a surprising amount of people will see value in your product, get to the end of their free trial, upgrade to a paid subscription, but still not be activated. You might call them a customer, but they are more like a qualified lead. I've been shocked on calls with these customers to hear that they are thinking of leaving because they think we don't have certain features we do, like integrations. Or they're only sending out proposals as PDFs, so they're missing out on the interactive fee tables, videos, e-signatures, analytics, and other great benefits they would get if they sent out their proposals through the product.

CUSTOMER SUCCESS

When people win proposals using Proposify, of course we want to hear about it, but we also want to hear if they're sending out a lot of proposals and not winning any. That's a useful data point, too, because it allows us to reach out and help them solve any problems that are keeping them from closing deals.

At this stage, it's worth building a team that's dedicated to reaching out to customers who look like they might churn and giving them some proactive care and love. Check in to see why they're not using the product. Is there an unused feature you could offer them that might solve their pain? It's not complicated; simply reach out to them and make sure they're getting the most out of the product that they can.

Within customer success, it's useful to focus on the customers who matter most, in terms of revenue. Logo churn (the accounts you lose) may matter less than MRR churn (the revenue you lose through churn). Let's say you lose ten customers; five of them paid $20 a month and five paid $2,000 a month. You would obviously much rather lose the $20 subscribers than the $2,000 customers because your MRR churn would be much lower from that first group than from the second. Invest in those larger customers as individuals. Better yet, look at net MRR churn, that is, the net amount of recurring revenue lost to churn *but* factoring in expansion revenue. In other words, if you can upsell existing customers into larger pricing packages, and you're gaining more revenue from this than you're losing to cancellations, you could have *negative* churn. Negative churn is the holy grail of SaaS, and means your company can grow exponentially.

Customer success is an extension of your sales team. Once an account executive closes a deal, she hands it off to a customer success manager who works to onboard, train, and retain the customer over the long term. In addition, the CSM looks for potential upsell opportunities, like having the customer purchase more seats or upgrade to a bigger package with value-added features.

Doing that, you are in a good position to reach negative net MRR churn.

SUMMARY

I'll repeat: If you're not growing, you're dying. I've discussed in detail the major lessons I've learned over the years when it comes to product development, marketing, and growth. As you grow your business, it becomes imperative to not try to do it all by yourself. The only way to grow customers and revenue, to pedal the bike up the hill at a faster rate, is to hire more people. With that comes its own challenges, which I'll discuss in the next chapter.

CHAPTER TWELVE

LEVELLING UP

You always know when you're watching a Quentin Tarantino flick. The witty dialogue, the incongruent music, the obscure film references, the extreme violence, the genre mashing; whether you're a fan of his movies or not, you have to admit he has a consistent style all his own.

In an interview, Tarantino once told the story of his meeting director Terry Gilliam early in his career and what the director told him that changed his mindset and gave him the confidence he needed to become a director. An intimidated Tarantino asked him how he was able to consistently make movies with his own unique style. Here's what Gilliam told him:

> It's not your job to create your vision. It's your job to have a vision, and then it's your job to hire talented individuals

and artists who understand your vision. You articulate it to them, and then they take your vision and they create it.

Immediately, Tarantino realized that what he lacked in knowledge of lighting and film stock and camera operation and makeup and special effects he made up for in having a clear vision of what kind of movies he wanted to make.

> I did have a vision, I did know what I want. I could describe it. That I could do, I can describe it, I can talk about it. That is what I know I can do. Pretty much since then, that's what I did. What you need to know is you need to have a vision and you need to know how to express it.

Most entrepreneurs start as doers, people who put their heads down and do the work. The irony is, if they're good at the work, it will bear fruit and grow beyond their capability to handle everything. We've seen that theme play out throughout this book. Usually, the entrepreneur understands when it's time to hire, train, and coach other people to do things on their behalf, but the transition is seldom easy.

Becoming a manager after being a maker is tough. I know just how painful it can be. Thankfully, I got plenty of practice (and made plenty of mistakes) at Headspace, so I was able to take those lessons with me into Proposify.

LETTING GO

One of the biggest mistakes we made at Headspace was to hesitate in hiring new people. We always looked at hiring as a loss. We focused on the money it was costing us in salary and benefits, rather than how we could use a new person to help fuel the business.

I knew from my experience at Headspace that this was a mistake, so in 2015, I started looking for someone else to manage all the day-to-day tasks around building new features and testing at Proposify. I knew Ricky would be perfect for the position; he's smart, coachable, and one of the hardest workers I know. At first, I only entrusted him with designing and testing, but his role evolved past that. I had to evolve, too, and give up micromanaging every aspect of the business.

As chief product officer, Ricky makes decisions for the product, and I now trust him to do that, even though we don't always agree on everything. We've figured out how to work together, and I give him the autonomy and authority to make most product decisions so that when I do feel strongly about a design choice, he usually considers it carefully and implements it. Usually when we meet to talk strategy, we talk about the big vision for the product and the key initiatives for the quarter—he takes care of managing the team and making my vision a reality.

The same evolution happened with Jennifer. At first, I wrote every post on the blog; it was hard to hand over the reins so she could author posts. I felt a bit uncomfortable when her writing style was different from mine, but, like Ricky, I had known Jen a long time—we'd worked together for decades, so I trusted her. They say you should never hire your friends, but for me it has worked out pretty well.

EXPERIENCE POINTS

When I think of growing in the role of a founder, I use the term "levelling up" for myself and for the people on my team. For the non-nerds reading this: when you're playing a role-playing game and your character wins enough battles and gains enough experience points, you've levelled up. Now you're stronger and can do more and take on more powerful enemies.

A founding team at an early stage startup looks and acts worlds apart from C-level executives at a big company. So, as a company scales, the founders and department heads need to level up quickly or get replaced. It's on me as the CEO to level up my leadership abilities so that I can, in turn, help my direct reports level up as well.

For example, I used to avoid having hard but necessary conversations with employees. Putting them off was a mistake, because the problem never went away; it always got worse the longer I neglected it. I've learned that having those hard conversations sooner and addressing the issue right away is better for all the people involved and the company as a whole.

I've levelled up in other areas of my management practices, too. Like many people when they first hire employees, I tended to create a "paint-by-numbers" type system for new employees. I provided specific instructions about how they were to fill in the colours, which discouraged creative problem-solving. I wanted to be the beginning and end point, and they could tackle the details in the middle. I never trusted them to take the project and lead it without me.

But over time, I evolved. I realized most good employees won't put up with the paint-by-numbers approach for long. They want to create their own to-do list and will be more motivated to actually finish it when they do. We've been pretty successful with that approach at Proposify—despite growing rapidly from twenty-four to sixty-three employees in 2018, we've only had a few voluntarily leave the company. Because we've created an enjoyable workplace culture, empowered people to do what they're best at, and left them to do it, we so far haven't had a problem with staff turnover.

COACHING

For a time, I struggled with what I should be doing and how I should be spending my time. I'm the CEO, but what is my job? In late 2017, I hired a business coach, Dan Martell, who has helped me continue levelling up. Dan helps his clients develop the skills needed to grow from a scrappy startup founder to a big company CEO.

Dan has been helping me figure out what my weeks and days should look like now. To Dan, the CEO has three jobs: (1) set the vision, (2) don't run out of money, and (3) hire great people and coach them to success. Everything else should be pushed down and delegated. With his help, I'm learning to work on myself the same way I worked on my business. It involves my personal, health, and business benchmarks, and being held accountable for what I say I'll do. In addition, he holds an offsite for his coaching clients in a different city three times per year. We sit down for two days and talk about our business problems, discuss solutions and frameworks, break bread together, and he introduces us to incredible entrepreneurs who are farther along than us. I've been fortunate enough to sit across the table from CEOs of billion-dollar tech companies and ask them about how they've overcome challenges.

Probably all the great leaders and CEOs have been coached. Surely Mark Zuckerberg has had some coaching since he was a student in Harvard until now, as the CEO of one of the biggest companies in the world. I think everyone should consider hiring a coach. To find the right coach, look for a specialist in your industry. A generalized business coach probably isn't going to help as much as someone who knows your industry inside and out. That's why I hired Dan Martell, because he's a SaaS business coach. He's rubbed shoulders with a lot of the best SaaS CEOs and founders, and he's built many SaaS businesses himself.

CHOOSING MY COMMUNITY

They say you're the average of the five people you spend the most time with. If that's true, you need to be selective about who you surround yourself with. I want to be around people I admire, people I want to be like. Some are entrepreneurs, others aren't. But everyone I choose to be around must be positive about life and passionate about their ambitions.

I have no room in my life for negative people, complainers, or energy sucks. Leaving the Jehovah's Witnesses meant cutting out a lot of these people, including my mother and sister. It even means avoiding some other ex-Jehovah's Witnesses I know, in the cases where our experience escaping a cult is where our similarities begin and end. Some ex-cult members do better than others.

I've been fortunate. Many others resign themselves to playing the role of victim indefinitely. The reason I left them behind is unique but the experience isn't. Other entrepreneurs often find themselves leaving connections behind as they make new ones. It's an adjustment, but judiciously choosing who you surround yourself with is one of the fastest ways to level up.

FOCUSING ON THE BIG PICTURE

Growing as a founder has meant learning to work *on* the business and not *in* it. Back in the early days, I did all the support, and I knew the product inside and out. These days, I can be stumped by questions from customers, and if I try to answer them myself, I can sometimes do more harm than good. That's okay, because I have people in customer support who are much better at handling these questions. But I still work to learn as much as I can about product, sales, and marketing because it's important I don't lose touch.

Gary Vaynerchuk has the saying "clouds and dirt." You need to balance having a big vision while also being a practitioner who still loves their craft and is willing to dig into the details. When starting out as a founder, you spend a lot of time in the dirt. As you grow, you need to adjust your view, look a little higher to see where the world is going. Your value now lies in being able to see what's coming next while also not being so high level you don't know how to execute. The hard part for a founder is to find balance between the clouds and the dirt. So how do you achieve this balance?

THE JOB OF THE CEO

As I've navigated this new world of big-picture thinking and left some of the day-to-day details behind, I've asked myself what "digging in the dirt" areas I can bring the most value to. Founders and CEOs have to let go of a lot, but what should they do? Here are my thoughts:

HAVE A VISION AND ARTICULATE IT

It can be daunting to be looked up to as the visionary in your company, but it is the CEO's job and one that can't be outsourced. How does one even create a vision? It's not out of thin air. Founders need to understand their market, and they do that by talking to customers regularly. Jump on calls, and go to conferences where your customers hang out to learn from them. You can learn how they use your product, where they're struggling, and what they're interested in. You can uncover their biggest pain points (which often turn into good ideas for future products or blog posts).

When you're starting a new company from scratch, hustling is important. Working as close to 24/7 as you can is important to get it off the ground. But as things start to get a little more stable and start to scale, it's important to carve out time for yourself. You'll wrestle with the guilt that comes with not being in the office all day. In practice, I've found that most employees don't really care. Sometimes they're even happier if the boss isn't walking around seeing everything they're doing or hovering over their shoulder. Leave them to themselves to manage the office and day-to-day stuff, and then, when you're in, your time can be spent on really valuable things like important meetings and one-on-ones.

I've read about founders going on long hikes and taking time to themselves. That might feel like just wasting time, but I've found that it's productive to take that time to get out of the weeds. It helps you clear out the cobwebs. Time away can also generate new ideas. While I'm working out at the gym, I might think of a strategy I wouldn't have necessarily thought of in the office, where distractions abound. The more time I pull away from the office and spend out of it, the more I can think strategically about the future.

As your vision for the company evolves, articulate it the best you can. I've found the best times to do this is at annual offsite retreats with the leadership team, in quarterly planning sessions, and at all-hands meetings in front of the entire company.

HIRE GREAT PEOPLE AND COACH THEM TO SUCCESS

You can't build a great company without great people. But how do you find them?

First of all, you need to be the lighthouse that draws the kind of people you want to attract. One of the best things we've done as a company was to define our core values—values we already demonstrate—and then base hiring and firing decisions on how well our people adhere to core values. We settled on four values: positivity, integrity, empathy, and drive. Our HR manager knows them well and uses them in our job ads. We use them to get the right people in the door. I review our core values at every all-hands meeting. If the founders demonstrate core values and only hire department leaders who do, too, it will naturally filter down across the entire organization.

When you have a great team, you can't just leave them to figure everything out on their own; you must give them direction and coach them to success. We do this at Proposify by setting annual and quarterly goals and then by running a weekly sync meeting to measure our progress. The weekly sync every Monday morning ensures the leader of every department is on the same page and is pulling their team in the same direction. We review the key quarterly initiatives and whether or not our teams are on track for finishing them by the end of the quarter. Then in one-on-ones with my direct reports, I can offer specific coaching for the individual, listen to their concerns, and ask what I can do to help them achieve their goals.

Just as a pilot would never fly a plane to a destination without checking his instruments to make sure he hasn't veered off course, you must also have a company scorecard and review it on a weekly basis. The scorecard tracks the health of the company across every department: product, engineering, marketing, sales, customer success, and operations. If a key metric, like sales velocity, net promoter score, churn, or marketing qualified leads is slipping, you can identify the problem in real time instead of waiting until the end of a quarter to realize you veered off course.

Your team members need to work well together, but that doesn't mean they'll be singing in harmony most days. Collaboration and cooperation are useful but you need some natural discord and dissonance, too. Chaos creates harmony. Let the natural pressures of problem-solving work their way through your teams, and you'll see the best products coming out of that process. Developers will fight the quality assurance people who slow their release schedule, while product managers push to get new features into customers' hands. Ultimately, the quality of the product will benefit from being honed in this high-pressure environment.

MAKE THE BIG DECISIONS

There's a last aspect of being a CEO, and that's making the tough decisions. Your third job is to not run out of money, and on a practical level, that may mean doing whatever it takes to allow the company to thrive. It could mean you need to kill a project that's going nowhere, merge departments, or make layoffs. It could mean raising additional capital at unfavourable terms, taking on debt, or selling the company at low valuation. It could mean firing your top executive and friend. It could mean firing yourself. As I said earlier in this book, entrepreneurship isn't sexy. It means sometimes, no matter how hard you try to do the right thing, people will hate you. And it means that whether you succeed or fail, it's on you. This is the game. This is what you signed up for.

CHAPTER THIRTEEN

FROM CHAOS TO CONQUEST

I grew up in a co-op housing project in the small town of Cole Harbour, Nova Scotia. Since the houses were all attached to each other, we were pretty close to most of our neighbours, both literally and figuratively. I remember one day in the backyard, my parents were having a conversation with one of the next-door neighbours, Sandra. Sandra had a daughter named Jackie. That day, Jackie found a bug in her dresser drawer. She screamed out the window, "Mom, there's a bug in my drawer!" Without missing a beat, her mother yelled back with a shrill holler, "Oh, everybody's got bugs, Jackie!"

From then on it became a saying in my household. For example, when gossip revealed that a Jehovah's Witness family, whom we had assumed was as happy and upright as they appeared, was being upended due to alcoholism, abuse, infidelity, or some other indignity, my dad would shake his head: "Everybody's got bugs, Jackie."

People who don't know me may look at who I am today without realizing what I've been through. And the same may be true for you, too. As humans, we tend to overemphasize our own plight and disregard the other person, assuming their life must be better than ours, without considering the struggles they may have endured to be here with us. But everybody's got bugs.

When you get all the different parts of your life running well and working together, the whole becomes greater than the sum of its parts. The last couple of years have been great from a business standpoint, and also personally. I married Christina, the love of my life, and I've greatly improved my physical, mental, and emotional health. Life isn't perfect—it never is—but I'm no longer in a constant state of chaos, and that feels really fucking good.

RELATIONSHIPS

Some parts came together easily and some have been more challenging, but I'm amazed to have come so far from the dark days before I left the Jehovah's Witnesses.

One of the best outcomes has been meeting Christina. After my excruciating relationship with Paula and a few reckless dating years afterwards, I had almost given up on love, but then met Christina in 2016 and two years later we are still best friends. She's a great stepmom to my boys, Micah and Ty, and we're excited to be a family. I also enjoy a good relationship with Alex, my stepdaughter. Now a young woman in college, I'm proud of the person she has become.

Navigating my relationship with my mother wasn't quite as successful. We did reconnect, and I tried hard to create a civil relationship with clear boundaries so she could see her grandchildren and we could all spend a little time together. Unfortunately, it didn't last; I think she felt guilty for spending time with me, the apostate. I'm sure she was pressured by the church to continue shunning me. In fact, she once told me she was sure my sister had done the right thing by shunning me for the last six years. It hurt to hear that. I lashed out and said some angry things about it, and that sealed it. We don't speak with each other anymore.

It's hard because she was a great mother to me growing up and always told me I could be anything I wanted. Without the confidence she instilled in me, I wouldn't be the person I am today. I hope she awakens from cult indoctrination one day, but I try not to think about it too often, because it's too painful to have this woman, my mother and once greatest supporter, hate me for what I don't believe in.

FINANCES

My financial situation improved greatly after we got secondary capital. I'm debt-free and have enough to invest, build a house, and have some level of security and stability. It's certainly a far cry from the days not too long ago of trying to borrow rent money from my aunt. We don't know yet if we'll run the company for the next twenty years, get bought out, or go public someday; but even if the company went bust tomorrow, we'd feel like we got something valuable from it.

Still, we're always looking toward the future. In 2018 we passed $5 million in annual recurring revenue. We're on the road to $10 million and beyond. It remains to be seen whether we'll reach the rare achievement of $100 million one day, but it's good to set any high goal and try to achieve it—even if you come up short.

We're realizing, and maybe our competitors are realizing, just how big the market is for what we offer. Every company out there sends some kind of document to get agreement from their leads—whether they call it a proposal, quote, estimate, statement of work, pitch deck, or something else. Virtually every company sends them and has the pain associated with sending them or getting them signed. It's a fast-growing category in SaaS right now.

We've found that there are companies that will pay anything from $3,000 a year to $5,000 and $50,000 a year to use the software. If we can solve the problem of helping their sales team write proposals faster or close them faster, that price point works for them. If you do the math on that for our six thousand customers, that's on the smaller end of the market. If we had ten thousand companies each paying us $10,000 a year, that's a $100 million annual recurring revenue business—and ten thousand companies in the world is a pretty small amount. It's a huge opportunity right now and we're pursuing it relentlessly.

LESSONS

If you've followed my journey through this book, a recurring theme has been aiming higher than what you think is possible to achieve.

When I started as a freelancer, I didn't ever think I'd be where I'm at now. As I said in the introduction, maybe if I'd aimed a little higher I would have gotten here a little faster. I imposed limits on myself because I'm not highly educated and had just finished the graphic design course at a community college. Where I live in Halifax, we're geographically isolated. I grew up thinking, "I live in Halifax, Nova Scotia. How far can I go?" I had no idea what was possible.

I also had no way to think about it. Due to the nature of my religious upbringing, I had limited critical-thinking ability. I couldn't learn critical thinking until I broke away.

Looking back, I realize none of that stuff matters. Maybe it's easier to get started if you've got a well-connected family and attend the best schools, but in the end what matters is the person and how ambitious, hardworking, talented, and smart they are. Sometimes, having limits can actually push you to work harder than people who have it a little bit easier. That was true in my case, and I have achieved more than I ever thought I could achieve.

Not everyone wants what I wanted. Plenty of people want to keep a steady job, watch three hours of Netflix a night, play on a softball team, and take an all-inclusive trip to Mexico once a year. That's what they really want, and that's fine, too. This book isn't for them, though. It's for entrepreneurs, and my advice to you is to think bigger than you are now. Don't impose limits on yourself. You'll find that all of the limits are artificial. Anybody can achieve this if they have the patience and grit, and are prepared to work their ass off for a decade or more. It's never too early, but it's also never too late.

BE A TENACIOUS VISIONARY

It's very easy to be talked out of your goals. Don't let it happen. I didn't. Like a lot of entrepreneurs, I'm stubborn. There were times when it might have been smarter to change course, but I stuck with it. I think you have to. If you're the kind of person that gives up too easily, you just won't make it.

Instead, go ahead and be a visionary. It's okay to have a grandiose vision. Design the product you want to use, and worry later about how to make that a reality. Stop looking at the logistics of it and imagine you had a magic wand. If you had a magic wand, what would you create? It might seem impossible. I'm sure all the engineers at Apple thought the iPhone was impossible. When they actually sat down and worked it out, though, they realized it was just hard, not impossible. It could be built. On a smaller scale, I found the same true with Proposify. For years I sat on the idea because I didn't think it could be made; but after I hired Jonathan, he showed me that it could be made—I just needed to find the right people to help me.

MAKE THE LEAP

If you're reading this book and you haven't made the leap to becoming an entrepreneur, but you want to, you can take it step by step. You don't need to go all in right away. You'll probably be working from nine to five for your job and doing a lot of work in the evenings or on the weekends on your vision, but that's fine. There are a lot of hours in the day outside of your working hours—plenty of time to work on your dream.

If you have a skill in high demand that people will pay for, going out on your own to freelance is the easiest, most painless bridge to becoming an entrepreneur. If you're a good writer, a consultant, or strategist, find one or two people to pay you for a month to do that, and that gives you time to get out on your own and start selling the same service to other people.

It won't always be easy. You might get sick. A family member might get sick. You might have financial hardships. Life can throw a lot at you. My journey to becoming an entrepreneur took me through a destructive period before I could rise up from the ashes. It's not an uncommon trajectory; it's just part of the process.

Hopefully, some of the stories and strategies in this book will help you avoid some of my mistakes. Or maybe they will be therapeutic and cathartic to come back to when you're weathering your own personal challenges. At the very least, you'll know you're not alone. Like me, you can turn it around.

Just three years ago, when I wrote down my goals—what I wanted professionally and what my perfect life would look like—it seemed impossible. Today, I'm there.

Experience tells me that the same is possible for you.

REFERENCES

"Freelancers Predicted to Become the U.S. Workforce Majority Within a Decade, with Nearly 50 percent of Millennial Workers Already Freelancing, Annual 'Freelancing in America' Study Finds," News release, press@upwork.com, October 17, 2017.

"Jehovah's Prophet," JWFacts.com, www.jwfacts.com/watchtower/jehovahs-prophet.php.

Alyson Shontell, "The Founder of a $50 Million Startup Just Sold His Company—And He Didn't Make a Dime," *Business Insider*, April 13, 2015, https://www.businessinsider.com/get-satisfaction-founder-says-he-got-nothing-when-company-was-acquired-2015-4.

Chris Von Wilpert, "Sumo Growth Study: How MailChimp Makes $400M Revenue," Sumo, October 9, 2018, https://sumo.com/stories/mailchimp-marketing.

David Heinemeier Hansson, "The Deal Jeff Bezos Got on Basecamp," Signal v. Noise, July 27, 2017, https://m.signalvnoise.com/the-deal-jeff-bezos-got-on-basecamp-b7a1cb39179e.

Irfan Ahmad, "Digital Marketing and the Rise of Video," *Social Media Today*, January 24, 2018, https://www.socialmediatoday.com/news/digital-marketing-and-the-rise-of-video-infographic/515408/.

Jordan T. McBride, "Monetization Matters for SaaS Growth," Price Intelligently, February 11, 2016, https://www.priceintelligently.com/blog/monetization-matters-for-saas-growth.

ABOUT THE AUTHOR

KYLE RACKI is the cofounder and CEO of Proposify, a software as a service (SaaS) company based in Halifax, Nova Scotia, Canada, which currently serves more than six thousand customers worldwide. He started his first business, a web design company, at age twenty-four and sold it after five years. Kyle has blogged extensively about his journey through the ups and downs of entrepreneurship and was the subject of a 2016 article in *TIME* magazine. He loves going to boot camp classes, swimming in the ocean, and spending time with his wife, Christina, and his two sons, Micah and Ty.

ACKNOWLEDGMENTS

Writing a book has been a dream of mine ever since grade six, when, as a class project, I had to interview someone with the job I wanted when I grew up: an author. My teacher was able to track down Lesley Choyce, a local novelist and poet. My interviewing skills were probably as unpolished as they are now when I interview guests on my podcast, but it was kind of Lesley to show up and answer a few questions from an eleven-year-old.

First of all, I want to thank my beautiful wife, Christina, for her love and support. I know it was hard not to talk to me when I had my head down working on this. Go on now and finish what you were going to tell me; I'm listening.

Thank you to my boys, Micah and Ty, for all the ways you fill my heart with love and laughter.

To my business partner, Kevin Springer, I wouldn't be in this position without you. Thank you for convincing me our product was going to be a winner when even I stopped believing it. We've had a wild journey; let's keep it going.

Ricky Ferris, thanks for following me into business and being the only person to celebrate my thirtieth birthday when I was at my loneliest.

Jonathan Down, thanks for never backing down when I threw crazy technical challenges at you. You helped me realize my vision I had long thought was impossible.

Jennifer Faulkner, thanks for building a world-class brand with me, pushing back when you disagree with me, and throwing a great Halloween party. *Ding.*

Joel Kelly, thanks for accepting my coffee invite when I was at my most confused and terrified, and for being there for me when I needed a friend. You were instrumental in my recovery.

Dan Martell, thank you for helping me level up and become the leader I never thought I would be, and Ben Yoskovitz, for your continued support, advice, and guidance over the years.

To the people at Scribe who helped bring my book to life,

I want to thank my publishing manager, Ellie Cole, my scribe, Sheila Trask, my outliner, Karla Bynum, creative director, Erin Tyler, and illustrator, Daniel Andersen.

To my eighth-grade teacher, Sheri Gaetz-MacCabe, thank you for telling me you thought I was better than how I was behaving.

To the ones who told me I couldn't, you made me fight harder, so in a weird way, thank you.

Finally, I want to mention people in the community who believed in me or inspired me in some way; Andrew Breen, Lloyd Evans, Katelyn Bourgoin, Ross Simmonds, Greg Poirier, David Howe, Rob Hansen, Marcus Murphy, M.J. MacKinnon, Patrick Hankinson, John Risley, Brendan Paddick, Bill Wilson, Peter Moreira, Permjot Valia, Ken Lee, Evan Radisic, Charlotte Murray, Tim Simony, and Rick Smith.

Made in the USA
Lexington, KY
30 January 2019